OCR
RECOGNISING ACHIEVEMENT

Achieve!
GCSE Spanish Skills

Terry Murray
Series Editors: Steven Crossland and Caroline Woods

Hodder & Stoughton
A MEMBER OF THE HODDER HEADLINE GROUP

Orders: please contact Bookpoint Ltd, 130 Milton Park, Abingdon, Oxon OX14 4SB. Telephone: (44) 01235 827720, Fax: (44) 01235 400454. Lines are open from 9.00–6.00, Monday to Saturday, with a 24 hour message answering service. Email address: orders@bookpoint.co.uk

British Library Cataloguing in Publication Data
A catalogue record for this title is available from The British Library

ISBN 0 340 80106 9

First published 2001
Impression number   10 9 8 7 6 5 4 3 2 1
Year   2005 2004 2003 2002 2001

Typeset by Fakenham Photosetting Ltd, Fakenham, Norfolk NR21 8NN
Printed in Great Britain for Hodder & Stoughton Educational, a division of Hodder Headline Plc, 338 Euston Road, London NW1 3BH by Martins the Printers Ltd, Berwick-upon-Tweed.

Contents

Introduction   v

1 Overview of the OCR GCSE Spanish examination   1

2 Listening – general hints, example exercises, answers and tips   9

3 Reading – general hints, example exercises, answers and tips   28

4 Speaking – general hints, example exercises, sample answers and tips   49

5 Writing – general hints, example exercises, sample answers and tips, coursework   66

6 Grammar – essential points of Spanish grammar   79

7 Practice examination paper (all components) with answers   97

Appendix – Listening chapter transcript, Speaking chapter transcript.   130
Practice examination transcript.   147

Introduction

To the Student

This book has been written to give you help and practice in preparing for your OCR (Oxford Cambridge and RSA Examinations) GCSE Spanish exam. The book offers you advice and practice on the four language skills of listening, reading, speaking and writing. You will of course have been practising these skills with your teacher and using your textbook, but the purpose of this book is to prepare you specifically for the OCR examination that you will probably be taking in the summer term of Year 11.

As well as being language teachers, the authors of the book are principal examiners for the OCR examination. You can therefore be confident that the advice you read here and the exercises you practise will be very relevant to the examination you will be taking in Year 11. The authors are very familiar with the demands of the examination and the type of errors that candidates regularly make and which may well prevent them reaching grades of which they are capable. The authors can therefore warn you of the pitfalls and how you can best tackle the separate parts of the examination.

Will you be attempting the Foundation or the Higher Tier papers? As you know, you can mix the tiers in different papers in the OCR examination. You might, for instance, want to attempt the Foundation tier in listening but the Higher Tier in reading. In any case, you do not have to decide until later on in Year 11. The authors hope that this book will help you decide which tier to attempt in each component. It is important to attempt the tier with which you feel comfortable but not to undersell yourself by attempting Foundation when you might be capable of Higher. But whichever tier you finally choose in each paper, you will want to achieve the best possible grade. You can reach Grade C even if you only attempt Foundation Tier papers in each component. But you can only reach Grade B if you attempt at least one Higher Tier paper.

This book will give you tips for tackling all the different types and levels of questions which you will meet in the examination. You will find sample exercises for each. Try the exercises, then check the ansers to see how you did and read the hints carefully. Towards the end of the book (starting on page 97) you will find a set of sample papers which you can attempt as if you were doing the examination. Your teacher may ask you to do these in class under exam conditions.

Learning to master a language is to a large extent a matter of confidence, so the more practice you get, in all skill areas, the more your confidence will grow. It is also essential to understand the grammar of a foreign language. This is an aspect of language learning which students sometimes dislike or find difficult. But grammar can in fact be interesting and it provides the key to understanding how the language is formed. We hope that you will find that the grammar section in this book will explain grammar clearly and help you to understand it – perhaps even to like it!

You will need to learn key vocabulary as well. Much of this you have been learning since your first Spanish lessons, but you need to be very confident of certain key words and phrases.

In addition to using the pages of this book, you can access the OCR website at http://www.ocr.org.uk where you can study and download vocabulary lists.

We hope you will find this book useful in preparing you for your GCSE exam. Good luck!

To the Teacher

You are most likely to be using this guide alongside the course book used by your pupils. The aim of the book is specifically to prepare candidates for the OCR GCSE Spanish exam. Achievement at all grades is targeted but the intention is to encourage pupils to reach Grade C at Foundation or Grade A at Higher.

Each of the units covering the four skills (chapters 2 to 5) gives practice and advice in the different exercise types set in the OCR exam. These are based on exercises which have been set in previous exams, but the practice exam section (chapter 7) contains entirely new material.

The book is designed to be used either by you, as a teacher, with your Year 10 or Year 11 classes, or by the pupils working individually. As such, it will obviously also be of use as a resource for pupils to work on if classes are being supervised by a cover teacher. Pupils can, if you wish, be encouraged to purchase their own copy for home study.

It is not intended that pupils should write answers in this book – in any case, there is not always enough space for writing answers, although we have tried to reproduce the style of the examination papers. Pupils should therefore be asked to write answers on blank paper.

There are pages on the OCR website containing vocabulary lists. Your students should be encouraged to consult and download this information themselves.

You may wish to use the practice exam section as a final "mock" before the exam or it could of course be used as an exam at any stage in Year 11. However you use it, the authors hope that you and your pupils find it useful and will achieve the results that you have hoped for.

There are companion books in the series for German and French GCSE with OCR.

1 – Overview of the OCR GCSE Spanish examination

Your OCR GCSE Spanish exam consists of four different parts or components: a speaking test, a test of listening comprehension, one of reading comprehension and one of writing (which could either be in the form of an exam or in coursework done during your GCSE course). Each of these is worth the same proportion of marks, i.e. each component is worth 25% of the final total.

You will probably take the speaking test (or "oral") first, then your listening exam – these two are likely to be before the week's holiday in June. After the June holiday you will have your reading exam and your writing exam (unless you do coursework).

Your Spanish teacher will almost certainly be the examiner in your oral exam. He or she will either mark it himself or herself or will send off the test to be marked by an external examiner. Whichever marking system is chosen, your test will be marked according to the same mark scheme. Your teacher's marking will be checked by an examiner and the mark you have been awarded may stay the same, may be raised or may be lowered. Your listening, reading and writing exams will be marked by examiners. If your teacher has chosen to do writing coursework with you, he or she will mark your work and, just as for the speaking, the marking will be checked and changed if necessary.

Once all your papers have been marked, your marks will be entered into a computer and your final grade will be calculated. This is done by adding together your marks in all four components and then converting them to a grade. But there will be a long process of checking papers during June and July before you receive your final result in August. OCR takes great efforts to ensure that the grade you are awarded is the correct one. They will also compare the grade awarded with the grade that your teacher expected you to get. Teachers usually predict your grade very accurately but there are sometimes differences. You might of course do better than your teacher had predicted. More importantly, your performance in exams can sometimes be affected by illness or by a serious personal upset. Again, such circumstances will be taken into account before your final grade is processed. If you are suffering from illness or are upset during the exam period, it is most important that you get an official doctor's note and that the teacher in charge of exams at your school knows of all the circumstances so that he or she can send off the required paperwork to OCR.

Exam papers are never the same from one year to the next, but there are always similarities because they have to be written according to certain guidelines set out in the exam syllabus. The following chapters of this book give you examples of questions that have been set in previous years in each of the four components. In chapter 7 there are some further examples, set out in the form of a new practice examination. The purpose of the next few pages is to give you an idea of the content of the examination and of each component.

Tiers

There are two tiers – Foundation and Higher. You will decide with your teacher which tier you will attempt in each component. It is quite possible that you will attempt the same tier for each component, but you are allowed to mix – for instance you could attempt Foundation Tier listening but Higher Tier reading. In each component there is a section which is common to both tiers (referred to in this book as "Section 2: Common Exercises").

If you attempt Foundation Tier papers in all components, the highest grade you can reach is Grade C. To reach higher grades you must attempt at least one Higher Tier paper. If you are unsure as to which tier to attempt and think that Grade C is likely to be your limit it is better to attempt Foundation Tier papers. If you attempt Higher Tier papers and do not perform well, it is still possible to achieve Grades C, D or even E. But the later questions on Higher Tier papers are difficult and you need to have confidence in your abilities if you intend to attempt them.

You will need to make up your mind about which tier to attempt in each component at the time that the school makes exam entries in February of Year 11. You will probably have done your "mock exams" just before or just after Christmas, so you and your teacher will have a pretty good idea as to what grade you are likely to reach. But don't forget how important those last few months of the course can be!

Course Content

For all four components, the content of the course consists of the following contexts and sub-contexts:

1 **Everyday activities** – home life/school life/eating and drinking/health and fitness.

2 **Personal and social life** – people – the family and new contacts/free time (social activities, sports, personal interests, weekends and days off school, entertainment)/making appointments/special occasions.

3 **The world around us** – local and other areas/shopping and public services/environment/going places.

4 **The world of work** – jobs and work experience/careers and lifelong learning.

5 **The international world** – the media/world issues, events and people/tourism and holidays/tourist and holiday accommodation.

In addition, the course content lists the grammatical structures you should know (see Chapter 6), the vocabulary you should know and the types of tasks you will be set.

LISTENING

At **Foundation Tier**, your exam will consist of:

Section 1 (30 marks)

- Five short, simple phrases in Spanish with instructions and questions in English and using visuals from which you select the correct answer or give a short answer in English.

- A further three, four or five exercises with instructions in Spanish. The Spanish is spoken at a steady pace. You listen for particular facts. There are different types of exercises such as multiple-choice, filling in a form, writing short answers in Spanish, matching words or phrases to pictures and so on.

Section 2 (20 marks)

- An opening exercise with questions and answers in English (5 marks).

- Two or three further exercises based on announcements, discussions or conversations in Spanish. You listen for details including the speakers' points of view. The Spanish is spoken at near normal speed and the speakers may hesitate or rephrase. Present, future and past tenses are used and opinions may be expressed. There is a range of different types of exercise.

The **Higher Tier** exam will consist of:

Section 2 (20 marks) exactly as on Foundation Tier above, and

Section 3 (30 marks)

- Up to five exercises of which the **last** will often have questions and answers in English.

- Longer, more complex texts spoken at normal speed, with hesitation and rephrasing and perhaps a little background noise. You will be required to listen for gist, identify the speakers' points of view, attitudes and emotions and draw conclusions. There will be a variety of different types of exercise and you will have some questions to answer in Spanish. The texts will include radio extracts, interviews, conversations, discussions and so on.

Both the Foundation and Higher Tier listening tests last for about 40 minutes. There will be five minutes' reading time before the exam starts. All spoken material is played twice and there are pauses for you to read the questions and give your answers. The use of dictionaries is not allowed.

READING

At **Foundation Tier**, your exam will consist of:

Section 1 (30 marks)

- Five short items with visuals and with questions and instructions in English. You select the answer from a choice of visuals or give short answers in English.

■ A further three to six exercises consisting of short texts including brochure extracts, letters etc. from which you extract particular details and there may also be a requirement to choose and copy words in the target language. There is a range of different test types as in the listening exam.

Section 2 (20 marks)

■ One exercise will have questions and answers in English (5 marks).

■ There are up to three other exercises from which you extract the main points and points of view. There is a variety of texts (e.g. instructions, e-mails, letters, brochures etc.) and present, past and future tenses are used. The texts are longer than in Section 1.

The **Higher Tier** exam will consist of:

Section 2 (20 marks) exactly as on Foundation Tier above and

Section 3 (30 marks)

■ Up to five exercises of which one will have questions and answers in English (5 marks).

■ Longer, more complex texts drawn from a variety of topics. You note the main points and identify points of view, attitudes and emotions and draw conclusions. Texts use a range of tenses and can be in the form of articles, letters, brochures, narratives etc. and there may also be a requirement to choose and copy words in the target language. There is a similar range of test types to that used in the listening exam.

The Foundation Tier paper lasts 45 minutes and the Higher Tier paper lasts for 50 minutes. The use of dictionaries is not allowed.

SPEAKING

The **Foundation Tier** test consists of Role Plays 1 and 2, Presentation, Discussion and Conversation. It lasts 10–12 minutes and is marked out of 50.

The **Higher Tier** test consists of Role Play 2 and Role Play 3 (narrative), Presentation, Discussion and Conversation. It lasts 12–15 minutes and is marked out of 50.

No dictionaries are allowed. All tests are recorded on cassette.

Role Play 1 is marked out of 8 for communication. There are four tasks, with instructions in English.

Role Play 2 is marked out of 8 for communication. There are four tasks, with instructions in English. One task contains an unpredictable element. You will have to respond to what the teacher/examiner asks you or says.

Role Play 3 is marked out of 8 for communication and should last no longer than 3 minutes. You narrate events using past tenses following a verbal and visual stimulus. You have to answer the examiner's queries and express and justify feelings and opinions.

The **Presentation** is marked out of 4 for communication only. You present a topic of your choice and talk about it for one minute. Your teacher will not interrupt.

Discussion and Conversation is marked out of 10 for communication and should last no longer than 7 minutes – 2 minutes' discussion of the presentation and 4–5 minutes' conversation. The discussion is based on the presentation that you have given. The conversation covers **two** of the following seven topics: **home life; school life; self, family and friends; free time; your local area; careers, work and work experience; holidays.** You cannot be asked questions about the topic which you have used for your presentation. You will not know in advance which two topics of conversation have been chosen.

Overall quality of language. All parts of the test except the presentation are assessed for this on the basis of the range and variety of vocabulary, use of tenses and your ability to apply the rules of grammar.

Examples of Quality of Language assessment bands:

19/20: confident and very accurate use of a variety of tenses. Wide range of structures. Pronunciation extremely accurate for a non-native speaker.
14/15: good use of tenses with only occasional errors. Pronunciation mostly accurate.
9/10: awareness of tenses but many inaccuracies. Some pronunciation errors. Hesitant at times.
4–6: very limited range of structures and vocabulary. Pronunciation approximate but understandable. Hesitant delivery.
2/3: very limited range of vocabulary. Answers brief and often monosyllabic. Pronunciation very approximate and delivery very hesitant.

WRITING (TERMINAL EXAM)

At **Foundation Tier**, your exam will consist of:

Section 1 (30 marks)

- Exercise 1: you are required to write a list of items in Spanish.

- Exercise 2: you write sentences by filling in blanks cued by visuals.

- Exercise 3: you write a few sentences of connected writing answering given points (usually five) in a message, e-mail, fax or postcard.

Section 2 (20 marks)

- You have to write a letter, fax or e-mail of 90–100 words in Spanish. You are given certain points to communicate. These will include using present, past and future tenses and expressing opinions.

- There is a choice of two questions.

Communication and the quality and accuracy of your Spanish are assessed in both sections, 30 marks for communication and 20 for quality and accuracy. The paper lasts for 40 minutes.

At **Higher Tier** your exam will consist of:

Section 2 (20 marks) exactly as on Foundation Tier above and

Section 3 (30 marks)

■ You have to write an essay, report or article of 140–150 words in Spanish. You are given certain points to communicate, using a range of tenses. You have to express and justify your points of view. "Justify" means: "give reasons for your opinions". Your Spanish should be of a good standard of accuracy and you should show style and a good range of vocabulary. You should make frequent use of more complex sentences and structures.

■ There is a choice of two questions.

Your communication and the quality of your Spanish are assessed in both sections, with 20 marks for communication and 30 for quality and accuracy. The paper lasts for one hour. The use of dictionaries is not allowed.

Writing Paper Mark Scheme

Foundation

Section 1, Exercise 1: one mark for each item clearly communicated in Spanish	8
Section 1, Exercise 2: 6 marks for standard of communication	6
Section 1, Exercise 3: 6 marks for communication as for Exercise 2	6
Section 1: Quality of Language: based on vocabulary, verbs etc. Assessed in bands	10

(Section 1 Total: 30)

Section 2: Communication: assessed in bands	10
Section 2: Quality of Language: based on vocabulary, verbs etc. Assessed in bands	6
Section 2: Accuracy: based on the number and effect of errors	4

(Section 2 Total: 20)

Foundation Tier Total: 50

Higher

Section 2: Communication, Quality of Language and Accuracy as above	20
Section 3: Communication: range, effectiveness and clarity. Assessed in bands	10
Section 3: Quality of language: assessed in bands	14
Section 3: Accuracy: as above, assessed in bands	6

(Section 3 Total: 30)

Higher Tier Total: 50

Examples of Communication assessment bands:

Section 1 Exercises 2 and 3

5–6: meets all or most of the requirements set.
3–4: some omissions in fulfilling task.
1–2: only very intermittent response to task.

Section 2

8–10: all points of the task communicated; personal opinions communicated.
5–7: main points communicated in sentence form. Additional details often communicated.
1: main points communicated in short sentences.

Section 3

9–10: communicates and expands on information; narrates events with no ambiguity; communicates and justifies a range of ideas and points of view; pleasant to read.
5–6: all points of task and opinions communicated in some detail; communicates a very clear message.
3–4: all points of task and opinions communicated; despite errors, communicates a clear message including past, present and future events where required.

Examples of Quality of Language assessment bands:

Section 1

8–10: basic range of vocabulary; some awareness of verb usage with limited success.
5–7: restricted range of vocabulary; short sentences communicate simple points.

Section 2

5–6: basic style of writing; past, present and future tenses used at a basic level.
3–4: sentences may be repetitive; some limited attempt at the use of more than one tense.

Section 3

12–14: wide variety of structure and vocabulary; verb tenses used with ease.
6–8: a range of structure and vocabulary; tenses used effectively but with limitations.
3–5: limited range of structure and vocabulary; tenses used at a basic level.

Examples of Accuracy assessment bands:

Section 2

3–4: more accuracy than inaccuracy; sufficiently accurate to convey a clear message.

1–2: conveys clear message despite regular errors; inaccuracy often obscures meaning.

Section 3

6: overall impression is one of accuracy, with very few major errors.

4–5: writing is generally accurate; errors do not significantly affect the meanings.

2–3: inaccuracy does not impede expression of a range of meanings.

1: the writing is sufficiently accurate to enable a clear message to be conveyed.

0: insufficient accurate language to convey the meanings.

Note: in *coursework*, each item is marked out of 30 marks of which 10 are for communication and 20 are for quality of language. In order to achieve a communication mark of 8 or better on an individual item, you should produce 400–500 words in the three items submitted, taken together. Furthermore, to achieve a communication mark of 7 or better you must cover present, future and past tenses in the three items, taken together. To score a communication mark of 7 or more you must express personal opinions and for 9 marks or more you must justify opinions.

2 – Listening

General Hints

Listening is a skill which needs to be practised. The more Spanish you hear, the better your understanding will become. Take the opportunity to listen to Spanish on TV, in films or on the radio. Don't feel disheartened if you can't understand it all – a vital skill is that of "gist understanding" where you can understand the general idea of what is being said even if you don't manage to pick out particular details.

The examination will test your ability to understand spoken Spanish using a range of types of exercises, examples of which you will find on the following pages. You will sometimes be required to choose one of three possible answers (multiple choice) or you may be required to match up something you hear with a picture of statement chosen from a series or to write answers in English or in Spanish.

Here is a check list of the main points for success in listening:

- **Study the example.** Given the wide range of question types set, it is vital that you study the example which is always given at the start of an exercise. You should familiarise yourself with the commonly used instructions such as *Pon una señal en la casilla correcta*, but it is often as useful to study the example, as this shows you exactly what you have to do.

- **Study the questions.** Use the time made available on the recording to study the questions. It is sometimes a good idea to highlight key words such as *dónde, cuánto, a qué hora* etc. You will always be given a little time to read the questions or study the pictures (you will hear the instructions *lee las preguntas* or *mira los dibujos*).

- **Note where the pauses are.** In the longer exercises, the pauses are marked on the question papers to correspond with the pauses on the recording.

- **Make use of both playings.** All recordings are played twice. You may well think you know the answer after the first playing, but always check when you hear it for a second time. In the same way, don't panic if on the first playing, you find it difficult to understand; when you hear the same material for the second time it is always easier to understand.

- **Write brief answers.** There is no need to write a long answer if one or two words are enough, provided you have given the required material. If for instance the question asks *¿Cuántos años tiene Pedro?* and you have heard him say *Tengo catorce años*, all you need to write for your answer is "*14*".

- **Learn how to answer questions about numbers and times.** As you can see from the above example, it is always best to write numbers in figures rather than writing the words. It is very common to be tested on numbers in the examination. Be sure you learn them!

- **Learn question words.** Be sure you know the meanings of *dónde, quién, cuánto* etc. and don't forget how the word *cómo* is used to ask for a description (e.g. *¿cómo es el pueblo?* – what is the town like?)

- **Don't worry too much about the writing of answers in Spanish.** Your Spanish must be understandable, of course, but you will not lose marks for small errors and details such as accents, plural endings, verb endings etc. At the same time, don't use English words in your answers. The idea is that your answers should be understandable to a Spanish person who knows no English.

- **Highlight key words.** As well as being clear about what question words mean, be sure to read them correctly in the exam. By using a highlighter pen you can draw your attention to them and thus reduce the risk of misreading them. This applies to question words in English questions as well – it's amazing how often candidates' answers in the exam show that they have read "When" as "Where". It's easily done if you're not careful. It's also a good idea to highlight the instruction which tells you the language in which you have to write as every year there are candidates who answer questions in Spanish when they have heard (and read) the instruction "answer the following questions in **English**".

- **Write clearly!** As in all exams, do your best to write clearly enough for the examiner to be able to read your answer. Write in blue ink only. Don't waste time writing in pencil then rubbing it out and rewriting your answers in ink. If you change your mind over an answer such as a letter, make your change perfectly clear so that the examiner knows which answer to mark. Never write one letter on top of another so that it could be read as two letters – examiners are instructed to mark such answers wrong!

- **Guessing answers.** It is not generally good advice to guess answers, but if you have no idea about an answer, make a sensible guess or, in the case of a letter selection exercise, pick a letter which you have not already used, rather than simply leaving it blank.

*Now let's have a look at the types of exercises which you **may** have in the exam.*

When you see this symbol, *find the relevant exercise on the cassette.*

When you see this symbol, *read the questions.*

Section 1: Foundation

The first exercise in the exam consists of five very short recordings. In each there is a question in English instructing you to pick one of three possible answers in picture form or to give simple answers in English. As always, you hear each Spanish phrase twice. The questions are based on simple material such as numbers and times, foods, forms of transport, directions and so on. They are intended to provide you with a simple opening exercise to give you confidence. Most candidates score the full 5 marks – but it does assume that you know this simple vocabulary, so be sure you have learned the basics!

Here is a typical opening exercise.

When you hear the pause signal, pause the tape.

When you hear the repeat signal, rewind to the beginning of the exercise.

Find Exercise 1 on the cassette

The first exercise in the exam consists of five very short recordings. There are questions in English instructing you to give simple answers in English. As always, you hear each Spanish phrase twice. The questions are based on simple vocabulary, and you have to listen to the key word. You should be able to score full marks in this opening exercise, which will give you confidence for the rest of the paper. To make sure of this, learn the basic vocabulary for each topic.

Exercise 1:   Questions 1–5

A Spanish girl is speaking about her plans for the weekend. Answer briefly in English.

> **Example:**
>
> Who is coming?
>
> .... *her friend* .... [1]
>
> The correct answer is **her friend**.

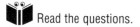 Read the questions.

1 Where are they going?

.... [1]

2 How will they travel?

.... [1]

3 What time does it start?

.... [1]

4 How much does it cost?

.... [1]

5 When are they going to the disco?

.... [1]

[Total: 5 marks]

In the next exercise you pick out one of three pictures for each question and tick the box. Notice the example: with listening exams there is always an example.

Find Ejercicio 2 on the cassette.

The second exercise in the exam consists of five very short recordings. In each you pick one of three possible answers in picture form. As always, you hear each Spanish phrase twice. The questions are based on simple shopping vocabulary, and you have to listen to the key word.

Ejercicio 2:   Preguntas 1–5

¿Dónde estás?
Marca una señal (✔) en la casilla correcta.

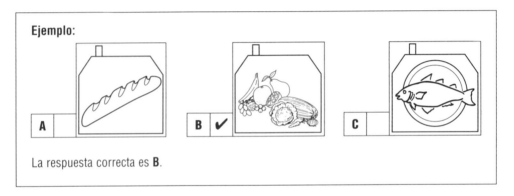

 Mira los dibujos.

Escucha.

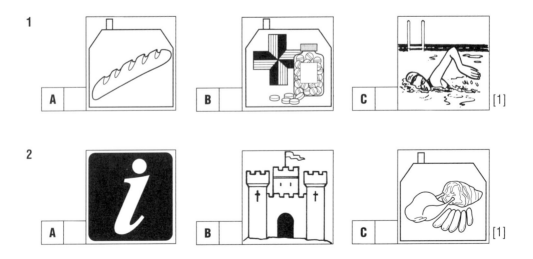

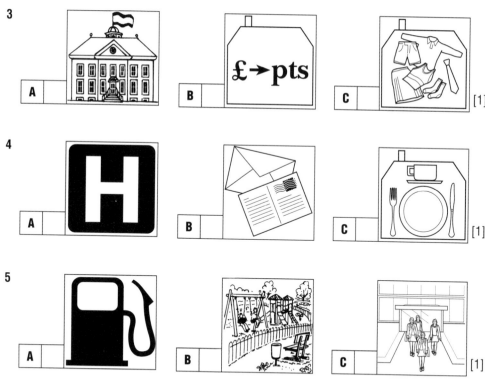

[Total: 5 marks]

In the following exercise a Spaniard is describing the different features of a town. You have to understand which feature is being referred to and write the letter in the box.

Find Ejercicio 3 on the cassette.

Ejercicio 3: Preguntas 1–5

Antonio describe la ciudad. ¿De qué habla?

Escribe la letra que corresponde.

Ejemplo: B
La respuesta correcta es **B**.

 Mira el plano.

Escucha.

El plano de la ciudad

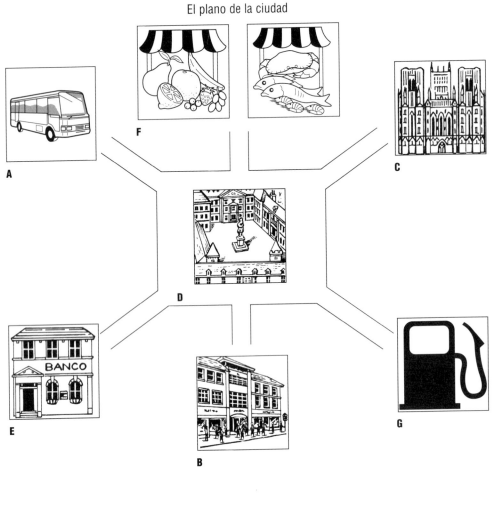

1 ☐ [1]

2 ☐ [1]

3 ☐ [1]

4 ☐ [1]

5 ☐ [1]

[Total: 5 marks]

In Exercise 4 you have to listen to the cassette and write in the words that are left blank on your exam paper. You are listening to a phone message and writing down that message. *Recado* on your exam paper means "message". *Apuntes* on your paper means "notes".

Find Ejercicio 4 on the cassette.

Ejercicio 4:   Preguntas 1–5

Estás solo(a) en casa de tu amigo español. Suena el teléfono. Tú tomas un recado para el padre de tu amigo. Haz unos apuntes **en español**.

> **Ejemplo:**
>
> Han llamado de   .... *La agencia de viajes* ....

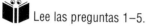 Lee las preguntas 1–5.

Escucha el recado.

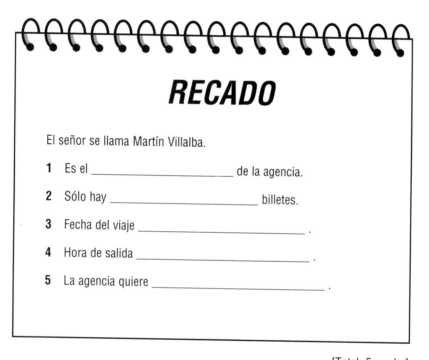

RECADO

El señor se llama Martín Villalba.

1 Es el _____ de la agencia.

2 Sólo hay _____ billetes.

3 Fecha del viaje _____ .

4 Hora de salida _____ .

5 La agencia quiere _____ .

[Total: 5 marks]

Section 2: Common Exercises

In Section 2, exercises are designed to test Grades D and C (although if you are entered for Foundation Tier, you will have to perform well in the Foundation exercises in order to accumulate enough marks to reach Grade C). The passages in this section tend to be longer than in Section 1, the pace is faster and the speakers will sometimes hesitate and repeat phrases in a different way, as people do in any language when they are speaking naturally.

You will not simply be required to pick out particular details as you do for the most part in Section 1. A very important skill tested is that of "gist understanding" – you will see examples below. You also have to show understanding of people's feelings and moods. Opinions are tested and tenses other than the present are used. One of the exercises has questions in English to answer in English.

First, an exercise with questions and answers **in English**.

Find Exercise 5 on the cassette.

Exercise 5:   Questions 1–4

You listen to a recorded message at your penfriend's house.

Answer **in English**.

Example: Where is the caller phoning from?

.... *hospital* .... [1]

The correct answer is: **hospital**

 Read through the questions.

1 How long has Oscar been waiting to see the doctor?

.... [1]

2 Oscar has hurt his . . .

.... [1]

   and his . . .

.... [1]

3 How **exactly** did the accident occur?

.... [1]

4 Where **exactly** on the Cáceres road was the accident?

.... [1]

[Total: 5 marks]

The next exercise is particularly useful because it tests parts of the body and medical problems, extremely popular subjects with examination setters!

Again the questions are in English so be sure to answer in English.

Find Exercise 6 on the cassette.

Exercise 6:   Questions 1–5

You will hear excerpts from conversations between a doctor and her patients.

Questions 1–4:   What medical problem is mentioned?
Question 5:   What advice is given?

 Now listen to the tape and answer the questions in **English**.

1 Medical problem.

_____ [1]

2 Medical problem.

_____ [1]

3 Medical problem.

_____ [1]

4 Medical problem.

_____ [1]

5 Advice.

_____ [1]

[Total: 5 marks]

The following exercise is invaluable because weather questions come up every two or three years. You require another section in your vocabulary book titled *El tiempo*.

Find Ejercicio 7 on the cassette.

Ejercicio 7:   Preguntas 1–4

En la radio: el pronóstico del tiempo.
Escribe la letra que corresponde.
No necesitarás todas las letras.

 Mira los dibujos.

Ejemplo:
Los Pirineos   F   D
Las respuestas correctas son: F y D

Escucha.

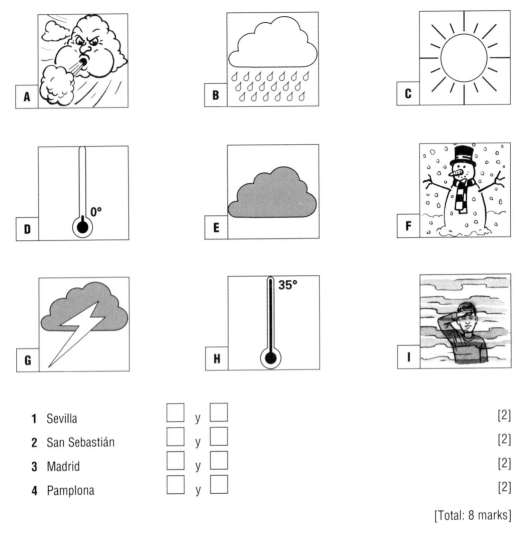

1	Sevilla	☐ y ☐		[2]
2	San Sebastián	☐ y ☐		[2]
3	Madrid	☐ y ☐		[2]
4	Pamplona	☐ y ☐		[2]

[Total: 8 marks]

Now find Ejercicio 8 on the cassette.

This is another extremely common exercise. You are given clues to a person's job and you have to say what the job is. You need another section in your vocabulary book for Empleos. Look at the question paper. Some words you might have trouble with are:

cuidar	to look after
fontanero	plumber
enseñar	to teach
los viejos	old people

Ejercicio 8:   Preguntas 1–5

Escuchas a unos estudiantes españoles que hablan de su futuro.

 Mira la lista de descripciones.

Escucha y escribe la letra que corresponde. No necesitarás todas las letras.

Ejemplo: **Manuel**

Soy Manuel. Me encanta el fútbol. Me entreno tres veces a la semana y juego todos los domingos. Voy a jugar en un club famoso.

La respuesta correcta es C. Manuel   **C**

Escucha a los jóvenes.

Futuros

A   Quiere cuidar a los viejos

B   Quiere trabajar con los niños

C   Quiere ser deportista

D   Quiere ser fontanero

E   Quiere ser mecánico

F   Quiere ser músico

G   Quiere ser artista

H   Quiere trabajar en una oficina

I   Quiere enseñar

J   Quiere hacer mucho dinero

Estudiantes

1   Susana   ☐   [1]

2   Yolanda   ☐   [1]

3   Alvaro   ☐   [1]

4   Patricia   ☐   [1]

5   Jaime   ☐   [1]

[Total: 5 marks]

Section 3: Higher

Higher Tier, as you know, gives access to Grades B and above. It consists of Section 2 (see above) which is also part of Foundation Tier, and Section 3. Examples of Section 3 exercises follow. In order to secure a good mark on this tier, you obviously have to perform well on Section 2. Although you can expect the Section 3 exercises to be more difficult than those on Section 2, it is important that you perform to your best ability on both sections in order to reach enough marks to secure the grade you want.

In Section 3 you can expect the Spanish to be read more quickly, sometimes imitating the style of radio announcements such as news bulletins, weather forecasts etc. Gist comprehension is used a lot in this section. There are almost certain to be a few words that you do not understand, but you must not let this put you off. Use both listenings so that you can understand as well as you can what is being said, bearing in mind the advice given at the start of this section to read the questions carefully, note the location of the pauses etc. You will be required to draw conclusions from what you hear and recognise points of view, attitudes and emotions. One exercise will have questions in English requiring answers in English – **this will be the final exercise in the section.**

Find Ejercicio 9 on the cassette.

Ejercicio 9:   Preguntas 1–10

En la radio. ¿De qué se habla?

Escribe la letra que corresponde mejor. No necesitarás todas las letras.

 Mira la lista.

> **Ejemplo:**
>
> *La respuesta correcta es: E*

A – Historia	G – Robo
B – Fútbol	H – Ejercicio físico
C – Accidente	I – Desaparición de una persona
D – Amor	J – Trabajos nuevos
E – Visita política	K – Dificultades del transporte
F – Lotería	L – Turismo

Escucha.

	Letra
Ejemplo	E
1	
2	
3	
4	

5	
6	
7	
8	
9	
10	

[Total: 10 marks]

In the next exercise, you hear people giving opinions about films and you have to identify the opinion from the list. In the list of opinions, *demasiado corta* means too short, *triste* means sad and *aburrida* means boring. This exercise asks you to recognise opinions and emotions and to draw conclusions, skills that are required if you are to be awarded grade A.

Find Ejercicio 10 on the cassette.

Ejercicio 10: Preguntas 1–10

Estas personas han visto unas películas.

Escribe la letra de la **opinión** que corresponde mejor. No necesitarás todas las letras.

> **Ejemplo:**
>
> *La respuesta correcta es L.*

 Lee las descripciones.

Escucha.

	Opinión
A	Violenta
B	Cómica
C	Recomendable
D	Para niños
E	Demasiado corta
F	Triste
G	Complicada
H	Para adultos
I	Estúpida
J	Histórica
K	Aburrida
L	Excelente

Ej	L	
1		[1]
2		[1]
3		[1]
4		[1]
5		[1]
6		[1]
7		[1]
8		[1]
9		[1]
10		[1]

[Total: 10 marks]

This is an example of the final exercise in the Higher Tier that has to be answered in English. It will be hard. It will require you to draw conclusions and will require a good understanding of what is being said.

Find Exercise 11 on the cassette.

Exercise 11:   Questions 1–5

You hear Ramón talking to a friend about his job.

Answer in **English**.

> **Example:** What is Ramón's job?
>
> .... *electronics engineer* .... [1]

Read the questions.

Listen to the conversation for the first time.

Questions 1–3

1 Describe Ramón's mood

.... [1]

2 What did his company choose to do?

.... [1]

3 What objection does he have concerning his new position?

.... [1]

[Pause]

Questions 4–5

4 What new request has his boss made?

.... [1]

5 What information does the boss not have?

.... [1]

[Total: 5 marks]

ANSWERS AND TIPS

Section 1

Tips

With all these listening exercises, follow this routine.

1 Listen to the exercise on cassette.

2 Check your answer.

3 Read through the transcript.

4 In your vocabulary book, write down any word you did not know. You may have to use a dictionary.

5 Listen to the cassette again with the transcript in front of you.

Exercise 1 Answers

1 cinema   **2** bus   **3** 8   **4** 400   **5** tomorrow   [Total: 5 marks]

Tips

It is essential to revise numbers, times, places in the town, directions and days of the week for this exercise.

Ejercicio 2 Answers

1 A   **2** C   **3** C   **4** B   **5** A   [Total: 5 marks]

Tips

While waiting for the recording to start, work out in your mind the Spanish for the items in the pictures.

Q.1: *Barra* means loaf, *panecillo* is a roll and *pastel* is a cake.

Q.2: *Salchichas* is sausages and *pollo* is chicken.

Q.4: *Sello* is a stamp, *mandar* is to send and *carta* is a letter.

Q.5: *Gasolina* is petrol.

Ejercicio 3 Answers

1 D   **2** A   **3** C   **4** F   **5** E   [Total: 5 marks]

You need to know the Spanish for all the places in the town. Why not have a separate section in your vocabulary book for these words? Your exam board produces a list of words that the Foundation Tier is based on. Why not ask your teacher for a copy of the list? Say you would like a copy of the Minimum Core Vocabulary, or download it from the OCR website.

Q.1: *Plaza Mayor* is the main square.

Q.2: *Estación de autocares* is the bus station.

Q.3: *Tienes que* . . . means: you must . . .

Q.4: *Se vende* means "they sell" and *mercado* means market.

Q.5: *Cambiar* means to change.

Ejercicio 4 Answers

1 jefe   **2** 2   **3** 24   **4** 07.35   **5** tarjeta de crédito   [Total: 5 marks]

Q.1: *Jefe* means chief or boss.

Q.2: *Sólo* with an accent means only. Without an accent it means alone.

Q.3: A difficult question. The speaker says in Spanish "the 23rd is a bank holiday so they'll have to travel on the following day". *El día siguiente* is the following day. Why not have a section in your vocabulary book for Time Expressions?

Q.4: *Vuelo* is flight and *dura* means lasts.

Q.5: *Tarjeta de crédito* is credit card and is tested extremely often.

Section 2

Exercise 5 Answers

1 an hour   **2** leg . . . back   **3** lorry hit him   **4** traffic lights   [Total: 5 marks]

Every year there are candidates who give correct answers and get no marks because they use the wrong language. The rule is: if the question is in Spanish, answer in Spanish; if the question is in English, answer in English.

Q.1: *Todavía* means still and *esperando* means waiting.

Q.2: *Parece* means "it seems", *roto* means broken, *pierna* is leg and *espalda* is "back". Why not have a section in your vocabulary book for body words?

Q.3: "Camión" is lorry and "chocar" is to collide.

Q.4: "Semáforos" is traffic lights.

Exercise 6 Answers

1 stomach   **2** headache   **3** cut herself   **4** eyesight   **5** stay in bed   [Total: 5 marks]

Tips

Q.1: *Me duele* means "it hurts". *Estómago* should go into your vocabulary book under Parts of the Body.

Q.2: *Dolor de cabeza* is a headache.

Q.3: The key words here are *cuchillo* (knife), *cortar* (to cut), *mano* (hand), *sangre* (blood) and *parar* (to stop).

Q.4: Two clues to the answer are given: *no veo* means "I don't/can't see" and *llevar gafas* means to wear glasses.

Q.5: *Guardar cama* means to stay in bed.

Get someone to test you on these invaluable words.

Ejercicio 7 Answers

1 H A or A H   **2** E B or B E   **3** C D or D C   **4** F I or I F   [Total: 8 marks]

Tips

To do this exercise you need to know that *nieve* is snow and *nevar* is to snow, *hay viento* and *hay niebla* mean respectively "it is windy" and "it is misty", *hace calor* means "it is hot", *hace frío* means "it is cold", and *hace sol* means "it is sunny". Other useful words often used in exams are *cielos nublados* (cloudy skies), *lluvia* (rain), *temperaturas bajas* (low temperatures).

Ejercicio 8 Answers

1 A   **2** H   **3** G   **4** J   **5** E   [Total: 5 marks]

Tips

Q.1: *Ancianos* means the same as *los viejos*, i.e. old people. *Jubilado* means retired.

Q.2: Words like *ordenador* (computer) and *informática* (ICT) regularly feature in questions.

Q.3: In this question the key words are *pintar* (to paint) and *hacer dibujos* (to draw).

Q.4: The word you might not know in this easy question is *lograr* (to succeed).

Q.5: The two clues here are *reparar* (to repair) and *taller* (workshop).

Section 3

Ejercicio 9 Answers

1 C   **2** H   **3** J   **4** L   **5** B   **6** K   **7** A   **8** I   **9** D   **10** F   [Total: 5 marks]

Tips

Q.1: Remember you do not have to understand everything. There are four clues to the answer: *muertos* (dead), *heridos* (injured), *colisión grave* (serious crash), *autopista* (motorway).

Q.2: The three clues to the answer are: *entrenarse* (to train), *instalaciones deportivas* (sports facilities), *clases de baile* (dance classes).

Q.3: In this question you need to know that *creer* means "to believe" but *crear* means "to create". *Empleos* means jobs.

Q.4: The key word here is *visitante* (visitor).

Q.5: Three major clues: *equipo nacional* (national team), *jugador* (player) and *partido* is (match).

Q.6: In this question, you would be lost if you did not know that *RENFE* is the railway system of Spain, that *sindicato* is trade union and that *empleado* is employee.

Q.7: The word *siglo* (century) appears frequently in papers and here it is the key indicator of the answer.

Q.8: *Buscar* is "to look for". This is a vital clue to the answer. You will need to be familiar with personal descriptions so do study every word in the transcript.

Q.9: *enamorado* (in love) and *sueños* (dreams) are the key words here.

Q.10: *El billete ganador* (the winning ticket) and *gran premio* (first prize) tell you the recording is about a lottery.

Exercise 10 Answers

1 C   2 K   3 F   4 D   5 A   6 H   7 G   8 I   9 B   10 J   [Total: 10 marks]

Tips

Q.2: *Al menos no roncabas* means "at least you weren't snoring." You should have been able to work out the answer even if you did not understand this part.

Q.3: The key word here is *lloré* (I cried.)

Q.4: *Nietos* is grandchildren and *incluso* is even.

Q.5: The key words are *peleas* (fights) and *sangre* (blood) but you should have been able to work out the answer from *brutalidad*.

Q.6: The key words here are *no es apto para menores* (it is not suitable for youngsters).

Q.7: You need to understand *seguir el argumento* (follow the plot) and *difícil de entender* (difficult to understand.)

Q.8: You do not need to understand the first sentence (It wasn't worth queuing). *Tontísima* means extremely stupid.

Q.9: The three clues here are *qué risa* (how funny!), *divertida* (funny) and *me reí* (I laughed).

Exercise 11 Answers

1 fed up/angry (but "worried" is wrong.)   **2** move/relocate   **3** no pay increase   **4** work abroad
5 whether he speaks other languages   [Total: 5 marks]

Tips

There is some extremely hard vocabulary here. You need to take steps to learn it as you can be sure that some of these words come up every year. This is what the transcript means:

I swear, María, I can't stand anymore. I am fed up with all this. I have done everything possible to sort things out. And my boss always asks for more.

When the firm decided to move to Valencia, I moved too and went through all the problems of moving house.

And, when I arrived, I accepted a job with a lot of responsibility for no extra money.

And now the boss wants to send me to work abroad. He doesn't even know whether I speak any foreign languages. In fact, I speak English and French. But I am not going to tell him that!

These are the words you need to write down and learn (in the order in which they occur):

jurar	to swear
aguantar	to put up with
harto	fed up
arreglar	to sort out
pedir	to ask for
trasladarse	to move
mudarse	to move house
al (+ inf)	on (doing something)
mandar	to send
ni siquiera	not even (a very good expression to include in your writing exam or coursework!)
el idioma	language
los conocimentos	knowledge

3 – Reading

General Hints

A number of the hints given for listening (see page 9) apply to the reading component, but the most important will be repeated below.

In your Spanish reading examination you will have a range of different exercises, some requiring answers in Spanish, some in English. You will also be required to match statements to short extracts, pick the correct answer from alternatives and so on. Usually at Foundation Tier it is purely your understanding of Spanish texts that is being tested, but at Higher Tier, in addition, you are required to identify opinions and emotions and draw conclusions.

The material may consist of simple signs, instructions, magazine and newspaper articles or letters. Texts may be printed, handwritten or in a word-processed form. You will see a range of examples in the following pages.

Here are the main points to bear in mind when doing the reading exam:

■ **Watch the time!** You will have 45 minutes (Foundation Tier) or 50 minutes (Higher Tier) to answer questions on several exercises, worth 50 marks in total. Time can go quickly and you need to work efficiently. Remember that the later exercises will generally be more difficult and will therefore take up more of your time. If you find a particular question difficult, leave it and move on but be sure to make a note that you will need to return to that question in any spare time that you have at the end of the exam. It is a good idea to have a quick look through the paper before you start so that you can see how many exercises there are.

■ **Study the instructions and examples.** At the start of each exercise you will read instructions about what to do. These should be familiar to you but don't panic if you can't quite understand what is meant, because the example, which always comes before the questions, should make it clear what you have to do.

■ **Read the material through first.** Read the whole text, letter etc. before trying to answer the questions. Read it quickly, without worrying about words that you don't understand (there are likely to be some) then look at the questions and try to locate the required information in the text.

■ **Read the questions carefully!** Use a highlighter pen to emphasise key words such as question words. Note how many marks are available for each question and how much space is provided for your answer. Look out for questions asking for more than one answer such as "what two things does he say about school" or in Spanish "*¿Qué dice de su instituto? Menciona dos detalles*".

- **Give full, but concise answers.** The examination tests your understanding of written Spanish, so you need to demonstrate how well you understand. However, there is no need to write long answers if brief ones are sufficient. Don't bother about writing complete sentences and express numbers in figures (e.g. 25) rather than words (twenty-five/*veinticinco*) but do be sure to write down everything you understand that might be relevant to an answer.

- **Beware of including incorrect information.** Despite the above point, do be careful not to add incorrect details to your answers. If you give a correct answer and then add information which is not in the text you are likely to lose the mark.

- **Answer in the correct language!** Every year there are candidates who answer in English when Spanish is required or (just as frequently) in Spanish when English is asked for. Even though your answer might show that you have understood, you will not be awarded the mark if you have used the wrong language.

- **Write in understandable Spanish.** As long as your Spanish is understandable, where answers in Spanish are asked for, you will not lose marks for errors such as poor spellings, missing accents etc. You do not, therefore, need to spend too long checking the accuracy of your Spanish, though it does need to be good enough to be understandable.

- **Write neatly and clearly.** This is an obvious point and applies to any written examination, of course, but you must write clearly enough for the examiner to know what you mean. It is particularly important to make any changes clear. If you change your mind, be sure that you cross out the answer that you do not wish the examiner to mark (don't simply bracket it). If examiners see two answers, they are instructed to mark the one on or nearer to the line. Be particularly careful with answers requiring a letter to be written in a box; careless handwriting can make an E look like an F or a C like a G, for example. Beware! If the letter you have written looks as if it could be interpreted in two ways, examiners are again instructed to mark such an answer wrong.

- **Guess sensibly.** However efficiently you have learned vocabulary, there will almost certainly be words in the exam texts that you don't know. Don't worry! It is quite possible that knowledge of a particular word is not tested in the questions anyway. However, your ability to understand gist, and to make a sensible guess of the meaning of a word from the context (i.e. what is around it) is an important skill of language learning and this will be tested in the exam.

- **Learn vocabulary during the years before the exam.** You are not permitted to use a dictionary in the examination, so regular learning of vocabulary during the years leading up to the examination is vital. You can access the core vocabulary on the OCR website at http://www.ocr.org.uk and you will no doubt have lists of words in your textbook. Test yourself regularly on the meanings of the words, or ask friends or relatives to test you. Work with friends preparing the same examination and test each other.

Now let's look at some example exercises. You will probably find the first few quite easy, but they become progressively more difficult. Try them for yourself then check your answers to see how well you did. If you do well on the Foundation Tier exercises, try the Higher Tier ones. This could help you decide which Tier to attempt when you do the exam for real. Read the tips carefully and note the advice!

Section 1: Foundation

The opening exercise tests your understanding of five short texts (sometimes simply single words) such as signs, adverts and messages. You are given a choice of three possible answers for each.

Exercise 1:   Questions 1–5

Answer each question by ticking one box only.

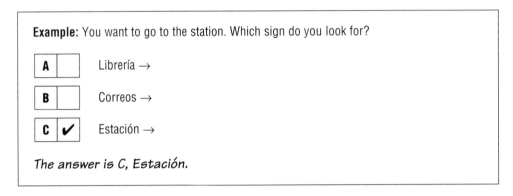

Example: You want to go to the station. Which sign do you look for?

A ☐   Librería →

B ☐   Correos →

C ✔   Estación →

The answer is C, Estación.

Now answer these questions.
You are in Spain. Which sign do you look for?

1 You want to buy some food.

A ☐   Mercado →

B ☐   Gasolina →

C ☐   Sala de juegos →

2 You want to post a letter.

A ☐   Correos →

B ☐   Estación →

C ☐   Plaza de toros →

3 You want to buy some shoes.

A ☐   Carnicería →

B ☐   Zapatería →

C ☐   Información →

4 You are looking for the town hall.

A ☐   Hospital →

B ☐   Centro de la ciudad →

C ☐   Ayuntamiento →

5 You want to buy a newspaper.

A ☐   Periódicos →

B ☐   Panadería →

C ☐   Estadio →

[Total: 5 marks]

The next exercise is a difficult one. You have to read the job advertisement and then fill in the blanks using words from the box.

Ejercicio 2:   Preguntas 1–6

Ves este anuncio en el periódico.

¿BUSCAS TRABAJO?
YO BUSCO CAMARERO/CAMARERA

¿Tienes entre 18 y 22 años? ¿Quieres trabajar como camarero/camarera?

Tendrás que trabajar los sábados y los domingos. Pago 400 pesetas por hora y recibirás muchas propinas.

Si te interesa, ven a "El Tulipán" entre las 5 y las 8 o llama al 416 43 38.

Pepe

Rellena los blancos para dar el sentido del anuncio. Escoge las palabras de la lista.

Ejemplo: Este anuncio ofrece _____ *... trabajo ...* _____

Pepe busca un(a) **1** _____ que quiera trabajar en un **2** _____ Será

necesario trabajar los fines de **3** _____ . Los clientes en El Tulipán son muy

4 _____ . Si quieres trabajar en El Tulipán, o puedes ir allá por la

5 _____ o puedes **6** _____ .

| llamar por teléfono | viejo | joven | fábrica | restaurante |
| mañanas | tarde | malos | generosos | semana | trabajo | escribir |

[Total: 6 marks]

In the following exercise you have to read a set of headlines from a Spanish magazine and match them to a page number.

Ejercicio 3:   Preguntas 1–10

Lees una revista española. Indica la página de cada texto. No necesitarás todas las letras.

Ejemplo:

Estimado Señor:
¡El precio de pan es un escándalo!   Página ..*11*..

---

1   Truenos y lluvia por toda España.   Página ......   [1]

2   ¡El equipo nacional ha perdido los tres partidos del concurso!   Página ......   [1]

3   ¡Este año las faldas serán más cortas aún!   Página ......   [1]

4   El nuevo estreno de Luisa Díaz es muy popular en los cines británicos.   Página ......   [1]

5   Ana Obregón se casa con Alfredo García.   Página ......   [1]

6   ¡Autopista nueva en el norte de España!   Página ......   [1]

7   Cinco maneras de ponerte en mejor condición física.   Página ......   [1]

8   Como cuidar tus rosas.   Página ......   [1]

9   El presidente de los Estados Unidos habla con el gobierno español.   Página ......   [1]

10 ¿Has ganado una fortuna? Lee estos números.   Página ......   [1]

[Total: 10 marks]

Lotería .... página 4
Salud .... página 5
Transporte .... página 6
Baloncesto .... página 7
Tiempo .... página 8
Moda .... página 9
Jardinería .... página 10
Cartas .... página 11
Películas .... página 12
Bodas .... página 13
Trabajo .... página 14
Política...................................... página 15

Section 2: Common Exercises

The following four exercises are examples of those which would appear in both Foundation and Higher Tier papers.

The first of these exercises requires you to read a letter then finish off an uncompleted sentence by choosing one of the phrases on the right.

Ejercicio 4:   Lee esta carta

Hola Lucy

¿Cómo estás? Mira, ¿Por qué no vienes a España a vernos en verano? Acabo de mencionarlo a mis padres y dijeron que sí en seguida. Creo que lo pasaremos muy, muy bien. Tengo muchos CDs nuevos que podemos escuchar. Vivo bastante lejos de la playa pero iremos todos los días en autocar. También mi hermana Juana se ha marchado a Alemania pero ha dicho que puedes usar su bicicleta. Será muy útil. Y si quieres mejorar tu español, todos mis compañeros querrán charlar contigo. Mis abuelos también quieren verte. Y hay un lago detrás de su casa. Mi abuelo nos enseñará a coger truchas.

Escribe pronto

Ana

Empareja las frases.

Ejemplo:

Ana quiere saber si ...*B*...

The correct answer is **B**.

A se divertirán mucho

B Lucy quiere visitarla

1 Ana dice que sus padres ......

C están de acuerdo

2 Ana piensa que las dos ......

D su bicicleta

3 Lucy podrá escuchar ......

E música nueva

4 La casa de Ana ......

5 Durante la visita de Lucy, Juana ......

F hablando con los amigos de Ana

6 Juana le ha prestado a Lucy ......

G está lejos de la costa

7 Lucy puede aprender más español ......

H a pescar

8 Al visitar a los abuelos, aprenderán ......

I no estará

[Total: 8 marks]

In the next exercise you have to choose a number and write it in the appropriate box.

Ejercicio 5: Preguntas 1–7

Ves un cartel en la playa. Se trata de problemas y peligros en la playa. Pon el número del consejo que corresponde al dibujo en la casilla correcta.

QUINCE CONSEJOS PARA EVITAR PELIGROS!

1 La arena caliente puede quemarte.
2 Los bebés deben quedarse a la sombra.
3 Ponte un sombrero.
4 Aprovecha la brisa.
5 Es peligroso dormirse al sol.
6 No bebas alcohol.
7 Usa una crema de buena marca.
8 No tomes el sol a mediodía.
9 Protégete los hombros con una camiseta.
10 Bebe refrescos con frecuencia.
11 Treinta minutos al sol es bastante.
12 Por si hay botellas rotas ¡ponte los zapatos!
13 Si ves la bandera roja ¡no nades!
14 Hay ladrones. Mucho cuidado con tus objetos de valor.
15 Ten cuidado con las rocas sumergidas si vas a nadar.

1

[1]

2

[1]

3

[1]

4

[1]

5

[1]

6

[1]

7

[1]

[Total: 7 marks]

Your knowledge of tenses is tested in the next exercise. You have to identify what was happening in the past and what is happening now. A difficult exercise.

Ejercicio 6: Preguntas 1–8

Lee este artículo y contesta **en español**.

Pilar Gómez
– entrevista exclusiva –

Pilar Gómez ha decidido vivir en España. Dice que gana mucho más dinero en España que en Francia donde vivía hasta recientemente.

Una de las estrellas más famosas del cine español, dice que su trabajo ahora le gusta muchísimo. Seguro que gana más que cuando era enfermera.

– Cuando yo era joven, quería ser tenista. Ahora las cosas han cambiado. Tengo casi todo lo que quiero pero falta una cosa: quiero ser madre. Me casé con Paco pero no quería niños. Ahora soy la esposa de Ricardo y él quiere ser padre.

– No me gustaba Francia: no me gustaba la casa en donde vivía. Estoy más contenta con el piso que tengo ahora en Madrid. En Francia me gustaban mis caballos: ahora no tengo tiempo. Cuando tengo tiempo libre, me encanta salir con amigos.

Ejemplo:	EN EL PASADO	AHORA
país de residencia	*Francia*	*España*

	EN EL PASADO	AHORA
profesión	1	2 ....
ambición	3	4 ....
tipo de alojamiento	5	6 ....
pasatiempo favorito	7	8 ....

[Total: 8 marks]

In this exercise you have to say what the weather is like in different areas.

Exercise 7:   Questions 1–5

You read the weather forecast in a newspaper.

Pronóstico del tiempo para hoy lunes

En Madrid capital se esperan tormentas con truenos y relámpagos. En Andalucía se anticipa tiempo lluvioso. ¡No salgas sin paraguas! Habrá chubascos fuertes. En Extremadura habrá vientos fuertes por toda la región. En Galicia habrá niebla por toda la zona.

En los Pirineos se prevén las primeras nieves del año. En Alicante el sol va a aparecer y hará calor por primera vez en muchos días.

What will the weather be like in these areas? Put the correct letter in each box.

1 In Madrid   [1]

2 In Andalusia   [1]

3 In Extremadura   [1]

4 In Galicia   [1]

5 In the Pyrenees   [1]

[Total: 5 marks]

Section 3: Higher

The texts are now longer. You have to understand gist, identify main points, recognise points of view, attitudes and emotions and draw conclusions.

The exercise which follows is one in which you have to fill in the blanks by selecting a word from the box at the bottom.

Ejercicio 8: Preguntas 1–10

Vas a viajar en avión. Lees este folleto.

VIAJERO: EVITA EL MAREO CUANDO VIAJES EN AVIÓN

ONCE CONSEJOS

Cosa importantísima. No bebas vino ni cerveza.

La noche anterior ¡no salgas! Vete a la cama a las diez.

Intenta charlar con alguien durante el viaje.

La lectura puede marearte: no compres revistas ni periódico.

Relájate: escucha un casete: escucha a tu cantante favorito.

Levántate de vez en cuando y da un paseo por el pasillo.

Toma tus pastillas muchas horas antes de marcharte.

Desayuna bien antes de marcharte.

Ponte en el departamento de no fumadores.

Las películas de a bordo son caras: pero valen la pena.

Si puedes, échate una siesta durante el viaje.

He aquí una explicación del folleto. Rellena los blancos usando palabras de la lista. No necesitarás todas las palabras.

Ejemplo: No bebas _____*alcohol*_____ durante el viaje.

Antes del viaje en avión, hay algunas cosas que debes hacer. Primero **1** _____

temprano la noche anterior: no te olvides de tomar tus **2** _____ . Al levantarte, toma

un desayuno bastante **3** _____ . Durante el viaje no **4** _____ Evita el

5 _____ de otros viajeros. Además hay otras cosas que deberías hacer. Es buena idea

6 _____ con tu vecino, **7** _____ si tienes sueño, **8** _____

música, ver la **9** _____ aunque hay que pagar y a veces dar una

10 _____ por el avión.

[Total: 10 marks]

película	foto	leas	dormir	alcohol	vuelta	humo	cena
medicamentos		acuéstate	hablar	fuerte	escuchar		

You have to answer the questions to the next exercise in **Spanish**.

Ejercicio 9:   Preguntas 1–10

Lee este artículo sobre una cantante italiana y contesta a las preguntas **en español**.

Mónica Dicaprio – corazón de oro

Entre conciertos, a Mónica le gusta relajarse en compañía de sus amigos: ella es una chica como los demás. Se viste simplemente. Siempre había llevado una espectacular cola de caballo pero estos últimos días se ha decidido por el pelo más corto que le da un aire mucho más joven.

Mónica trabaja como una loca. No ha parado desde que en mayo inició su serie de conciertos. Tuvo que suspender algunos de ellos a causa de una depresión, provocada por el estrés.

Su madre Rosa vivía en la pobreza en Cosenza, pequeño pueblo de Italia. Emigró a los Estados Unidos cuando estaba embarazada de Mónica. Sin embargo Mónica siempre se ha sentido muy orgullosa de ser italiana. Cuando quisieron cambiarle el nombre de Dicaprio a Perry, se negó.

Mónica es una persona de mucha compasión. Un ejemplo reciente es la visita que hizo a un gimnasta chino, Sang Lang, que se rompió el cuello realizando un ejercicio. Le han dicho que no volverá a caminar nunca más. Durante su estancia en el hospital, Sang ha tenido la foto de Mónica en la cabecera de su cama. Ella estuvo una hora con el joven y al salir, una multitud de periodistas le preguntó a Mónica cómo había ido la visita. "Ha sido una visita privada. Eso es todo lo que tengo que decir" dijo la cantante.

Ejemplo:

¿Qué tipo de persona es Mónica según el titular?

................*Es una persona generosa*..

---

1   ¿Qué tipo de ropa lleva Mónica?

.... [1]

2   ¿Qué aspecto de su apariencia se ha cambiado recientemente?

.... [1]

3   ¿Qué interrumpió sus conciertos?

.... [1]

4 ¿Qué sabemos de la vida de Rosa en Cosenza antes de ir a los Estados Unidos?

.... [1]

5 ¿En qué país nació Mónica?

.... [1]

6 ¿Qué opina Mónica de su origen italiano?

.... [1]

7 ¿Qué herida tiene Sang Lang?

.... [1]

8 ¿Qué sabemos del futuro de Sang Lang?

.... [1]

9 ¿Cómo sabemos que Sang Lang admira a Mónica?

.... [1]

10 ¿De cuántos detalles de la conversación entre Mónica y Sang se enteraron los periodistas?

.... [1]

[Total: 10 marks]

This is another exercise in which you have to answer the questions **in Spanish**.

Ejercicio 10:   Preguntas 1–8

Lee este anuncio y contesta a las preguntas **en español**.

LA FABRICA ROVI es el mayor productor de medicinas de España.
Buscamos un(a) joven para trabajar en nuestra fábrica en las afueras de Madrid vendiendo nuestros productos a clientes de habla inglesa. Dominio de inglés y francés esencial. Sueldo excelente y alojamiento organizado por nosotros. Mande sus detalles personales con un sobre franqueado a Juan Roelas, Fábrica Rovi, Madrid.

Ejemplo:

¿Qué se produce en la fábrica?

.......*medicinas*.................

---

1 ¿Cuál es la localidad exacta de la fábrica?

.... [1]

2 ¿Cuáles son las dos habilidades que piden?

(a) .... [1]

(b) .... [1]

3 ¿Qué dicen del salario?

.... [1]

4 ¿Quién encontraría el alojamiento?

.... [1]

5 Es necesario enviar dos cosas ¿Cuáles son?

(a) .... [1]

(b) .... [1]

[7 marks]

He aquí una carta de una candidata.

Contesta a las preguntas **en español**.

Stoke, 5 de mayo de 1999

Muy señor mío:

Me llamo Anita Sardá y he visto su anuncio en el diario de anteayer y quisiera solicitar el puesto en su fábrica. Tengo amplia experiencia con tal trabajo ya que llevo exactamente tres años trabajando en una compañía similar a la suya, United Medicines Ltd. Deseo vivir y trabajar en Madrid porque tengo mucha familia allí y hablo español perfectamente. Soy inglesa pero mi madre es francesa y mi padre español.

Vd. podrá pedir referencias a mi jefe en United Medicines Ltd y sin duda él confirmará que soy trabajadora y eficiente. Si Vd. quiere entrevistarme, mi día libre es el jueves y puedo viajar a Madrid aquel día.

Su empleo es de gran interés para mí y espero una contestación favorable.

Le saluda atentamente

Anita Sardá

Ejemplo:

¿Como se llama la candidata para el puesto?

........*Anita Sardá*........

---

6   ¿Cuándo se publicó el anuncio? **Escribe la fecha exacta**.

    .... [1]

7   ¿Cuándo empezó Anita a trabajar para United Medicines Ltd? **Escribe el año exacto**.

    .... [1]

8   ¿Por qué quiere Anita viajar a Madrid un jueves?

    .... [1]

[3 marks]

[Total: 10 marks]

In the next exercise the questions are in English and you answer **in English**.

Exercise 11:   Questions 1–5

Read this letter and answer from an agony column and answer the questions **in English**.

problema

Mi hija Lola es una pesadilla. Su ritmo de vida es acostarse a las cinco de la madrugada y levantarse a la hora de comer. Bebe alcohol y toma drogas. Nos ha escandalizado por su comportamiento y ahora voy a ver a un psicólogo. Vamos a celebrar dentro de unos días las bodas de oro de mis padres y mi hija Lola de 16 años se niega a ponerse un traje adecuado para la ocasión. Si la obligo me amenaza con no asistir. ¿Tengo que ceder?

Alonso (padre angustiado)

solución

Nada de psicólogos. Cómprate un coche deportivo. Será mucho más sano que gastarse el dinero en psicólogos.
Parece que tu hija sabe que ese acontecimiento es importante para ti, no para ella. Con su forma de vestir está expresando algo. Si tú te pones severo, ella también se pondrá así. El objetivo a conseguir es buscar una solución que os convenga a los dos. Si tratas de imponerle algo por la fuerza, vais a perder los dos. Para contestar a tu pregunta, sí, tienes que ceder.

Tía *Clara*

1 According to Alonso, what happened nearly fifty years ago?

.... [1]

2 What has Lola threatened?

.... [1]

3 What alternative to a psychologist does Tía Clara suggest?

.... [1]

4 What action by Alonso would have the worst possible result?

.... [1]

5 What is the final piece of advice that Tía Clara gives?

.... [1]

[Total: 5 marks]

Finally, another exercise in which the questions are in English and you answer **in English**.

Exercise 12:   Questions 1–5

You are reading the Problem Page in a Spanish magazine. Answer in **English**.

¿Mi marido tendrá celos de mi triunfo?

Soy banquera y me han ofrecido un puesto de trabajo en el que voy a ganar más que mi marido. He leído que esto crea dificultades en la relación de pareja, lo que me hace tener dudas sobre si aceptar o no el trabajo que me ofrecen. Por favor, ayúdame en este conflicto.

María Dolores, Bilbao

Es cierto que algunos hombres se sienten inseguros cuando la mujer gana más dinero que ellos. Pero esto no es motivo para que la mujer renuncie a tal oportunidad profesional. Mi consejo es que deberías aceptar. Lo más normal es que el marido se sienta orgulloso, pero si no, es problema de él y lo tiene que resolver él mismo.

Rosa Arija, psicóloga

Example:

What is María Dolores' job?

.................*banker*...................

1   What do we learn about María's new job offer?

.... [1]

2   According to the headline, how might her husband react?

.... [1]

3   What advice does Rosa give?

.... [1]

4   According to Rosa, how **should** María's husband feel?

.... [1]

5   What is Rosa's attitude to María's problem? Tick **ONE** box only. [✔]

| **A** | | María should not risk upsetting her husband. |

| **B** | | María should be proud of her husband. |

| **C** | | María should risk upsetting her husband. [1] |

[Total: 5 marks]

ANSWERS AND TIPS

Section 1

Exercise 1 Answers

1 A   **2** A   **3** B   **4** C   **5** A   [Total: 5 marks]

 Tips   Learn the commonly tested names of shops and town features.

Ejercicio 2 Answers

1 joven   **2** restaurante   **3** semana   **4** generosos   **5** tarde   **6** llamar por teléfono   [Total: 6 marks]

 Tips   Unless you know key words like *buscar* (to look for), *joven* (young), *camarero/a* (waiter/waitress), *propina* (tip), *llamar* (to call), you will not be able to complete this exercise.

Ejercicio 3 Answers

1 8   **2** 7   **3** 9   **4** 12   **5** 13   **6** 6   **7** 5   **8** 10   **9** 15   **10** 4   [Total: 10 marks]

Tips

Some of these are quite easy – you won't have had any trouble matching *lluvia* to *tiempo*, for instance, but you need to read the statements carefully to match *las faldas . . . cortas* to *Moda*, or *estreno* to *Películas*. You need to learn these key words: *trueno* (thunder – not train – that is *tren*!), *equipo* (team), *faldas . . . cortas* (short skirts), *estreno* (première), *casarse con* (to marry), *autopista* (motorway), *salud* (health), *moda* (fashion) and *boda* (wedding).

Section 2

Ejercicio 4 Answers

1 C   **2** A   **3** E   **4** G   **5** I   **6** D   **7** F   **8** H   [Total: 8 marks]

Tips

This is a very difficult exercise. Start with an easy one. In Q.3, if you know *escuchar* is listen, then you can match it to E. In Q.4, "Ana's house" can only be matched with a verb in the third person and the logical one is G. In Q.6, if you know *prestar* is "to lend", then D becomes the logical match. In Q.8, if you know *aprender* is "to learn", then look for things to learn amongst the matches; *a pescar* is the logical choice.

Ejercicio 5 Answers

1 4   **2** 1   **3** 3   **4** 11   **5** 5   **6** 14   **7** 12   [Total: 7 marks]

Tips

The word *ladrón* (thief) is tested very often in both listening and reading. Learn it! Although all the illustrations are clear, remember to familiarise yourself with the icons (you can access them on the OCR website at http://www.ocr.org.uk) because you will feel more confident when you recognise them. *Peligro* (danger) appears twice. *Arena* is "sand", *botellas rotas* is "broken bottles" and *mucho cuidado* means "great care".

Ejercicio 6 Answers

1 enfermera   **2** estrella de cine   **3** tenista   **4** madre   **5** casa   **6** piso   **7** caballos
8 salir   [Total: 8 marks]

Tips

You have to arrange the two rows headed In the past and Now. For Qs.1 and 2, there are two professions mentioned – *estrella* and *enfermera*. The word *era* (was) tells you that *enfermera* belongs in the past. Qs.3 and 4 test whether you know that *quiero* is present and *quería* is past. For Qs.5 and 6, you have to know that *vivía* means "used to live". In Qs.7 and 8 you have to know that *me gustaban* means "I used to like".

Exercise 7 Answers

1 G   **2** B   **3** A   **4** D   **5** C   [Total: 5 marks]

Tips   A weather question appears every two or three years so be sure to know your weather vocabulary. Although all the illustrations are clear, remember to familiarise yourself with the icons because you will feel more confident when you recognise them.

Section 3

Ejercicio 8 Answers

1 acuéstate   **2** medicamentos   **3** fuerte   **4** leas   **5** humo   **6** hablar   **7** dormir   **8** escuchar
9 película   **10** vuelta   [Total: 10 marks]

Tips   This exercise is about how to avoid travel sickness. It tests your ability to pick out words and phrases which are similar or identical to other words or phrases. For instance:

Q.1:   *vete a la cama* (in the text) and *acuéstate* (in the box) both mean "go to bed".

Q.2:   *pastillas* (in the text) and *medicamentos* (in the box) mean almost the same thing (tablets/medicine).

Q.6:   *charlar* (in the text) and *hablar* (in the box) both mean "to talk".

Q.7:   *échate una siesta* (in the text) and *dormir* (in the box) both mean "to sleep".

Q.10:   *da un paseo* (in the text) and *dar una vuelta* (in the box) both mean "go for a stroll".

Ejercicio 9 Answers

1 simple   **2** el pelo   **3** depresión/estrés   **4** pobreza   **5** los Estados Unidos   **6** orgullosa
7 cuello roto   **8** no volverá a caminar   **9** ha tenido su foto en la cabecera de su cama
10 ninguno   [Total: 10 marks]

Tips   This exercise is marked on communication and not on quality of language. Often one-word answers are sufficient to score yet many candidates fail to score by lifting irrelevant material from the text, often starting in mid-sentence, indicating to the examiner that they had not understood the text or the question.

Q.1:   Any reference to hair invalidates the answer to this question as does indiscriminate lifting of the text. *Se viste simplemente*, *simplemente* or even *simple* are correct answers.

Q.2:   *Una espectacular cola de caballo* is wrong. However, *su pelo* is enough to score.

Q.4:   You need to mention *pobreza* or *pobre* in your answer to score. *Embarazada* (pregnant) is wrong.

Q.5:   *América* is also a correct answer.

Q.6:   *Orgullo* is also a correct answer.

Q.7: *Cuello* is not enough to score. *Cuello roto, cuello rompido* and *rompió el cuello* are allowed even though the last two contain errors.

Q.8: *Caminar nunca más, no va a caminar,* or even the lifting of the sentence *Le han dicho que no volverá a caminar nunca más* are correct answers.

Q.9: *Ha tenido su foto* is insufficient to score. You have to communicate that the photograph was near or at the head of the bed.

Q.10: *Ha sido una visita privada* or *no mucho* do not give enough information. However, *Sólo que ha sido una visita privada,* or *nada,* or even *0* are correct answers.

Ejercicio 10 Answers

1 en las afueras **2(a)** inglés **(b)** francés **3** excelente **4** ellos – Fábrica Rovi
5(a) detalles personales **(b)** sobre franqueado **6** 3 de mayo de 1999 **7** 1996 **8** día libre

[Total: 10 marks]

Tips

This question is about an advertisement for a job and also a reply to that advertisement. If you write your answers in English you get no marks even if they are correct. In Q.1, *Madrid* was not enough for a mark as *afueras* (outskirts) was required. *Habilidades* in Q.2 means "skills". The three skills that score (any two from three) are *ingles, francés* and *vendiendo*. *Joven* is wrong. In Q.3, *sueldo* means the same as *salario*. In Q.4, *ellos* is correct but *nosotros* is not. In Q.5, *franqueado* is not enough to score. In Q.6, *hace tres años* is wrong. The question asks you to write the correct date. In Q.8, *para entrevistarse* is correct but *para entrevistarme* is not. Similarly, *mi día libre* is wrong but *su día libre* is right.

Exercise 11 Answers

1 Alonso's parents were married **2** Not to go **3** a sports car **4** if Alonso tries to force the issue
5 give in

[Total: 5 marks]

Tips

The reason why this exercise is in English is because this exercise tests your ability to draw conclusions from what you read. You will not score any marks by lifting from the text.

Q.1: "He got married" is inaccurate and insufficient to score.

Q.2: The only answer that is correct is the one that communicates that she would not come. Answers which do not mention this but mention that she would wear unsuitable clothes or would assist are wrong. *Asistir* means "to be present".

Q.3: "Buy **her** a sports car" is wrong.

Q.5: "do not give up" is wrong.

Why not spend some time writing the two passages out in English and then learning all the words?

Exercise 12 Answers

1 better pay than her husband   **2** jealous   **3** take the job   **4** proud   **5** C   [Total: 5 marks]

Tips

Again in this exercise you are being asked to draw conclusions. Your answers must be highly accurate and convey all the required information. For instance in Q.1, it is not enough to say the salary is good. You have to say it is better than the husband's. In Q.3, the word "advice" guides you to the word *consejo* in the text and you know you are looking in the right place. For Q.4, the word *orgulloso* (proud) is a much tested word. Q.5 tests whether you have understood the gist of the whole text.

4 – Speaking

General Hints

Speaking is a skill which you can practise regularly, both in class and at home. The more you can practise, the more confident you will become and this is the key to success in the speaking test. Remember that the first stage in speaking involves careful listening and concentration to make sure that you are answering the right question and providing the correct information.

As in the writing examination, your success in speaking depends on your familiarity with the language. It is vital to learn the vocabulary for each topic thoroughly and regularly **throughout** your course. You must **not** be tempted to leave it until the last minute! Try to learn only small chunks of vocabulary at one go – it's easier!

It is also very important to remember that although you should try to be as accurate as you possibly can, you are essentially being tested upon how well you can **communicate** and make yourself understood. It may sound obvious, but do try to sound as Spanish as possible! Try to avoid all English words and make a real effort to pronounce well. Remember that English words, even if they are the same in Spanish (e.g. *radio*), do not gain marks if you pronounce them in an English way.

For the speaking test your teacher will advise you to enter at either the Foundation or the Higher Tier. See Chapter 1, page 2. Don't forget that if you are aiming for Grade C or above you will need to be able to refer to events in the past, present and future tenses, so make sure you can manipulate time frames. You must also be able to express your opinions and give reasons for them.

Here are some points to bear in mind when doing your speaking test:

- **Arrive 5 minutes early** – don't arrive late and out of breath.

- Don't forget your **cue care** for the Presentation section.

- **Prepare carefully** in the 15 minutes before your test starts. You will have copies of the two role plays. If you can't remember an exact word think about the English wording of the question. Could you say it another way? If you are told to "ask for the bill", for example, and have forgotten *La cuenta, por favor* you could communicate this by saying *¿Cuánto es?*

- **Read** the scene-setting of the role plays – they are there to help.

- **Role Play 2.** If you have a task which says "reply to a question", think beforehand what you might be asked (in a hotel or camp site situation, for example, you are very often asked how long you wish to stay).

- As you go into the exam room – **smile!** This relaxes you. Breathe deeply and slowly. Remember your teacher may be as nervous as you! **Don't panic!**

- **Don't rush!** Speak clearly and if you need something to be repeated, ask. Learn *No entiendo* and *Repite, por favor*. It gives you a few seconds to think and keeps the Spanish flowing.

- Whether you do Foundation or Higher Tier you will have to prepare the following general conversation topic areas: **Home Life; School Life; Self, family and friends; Free Time; Local Area; Career, work and work experience; Holidays.** You cannot choose which two topics you do – your examiner will do this in the exam room. So be prepared to talk about all of them!

- **Overall linguistic quality.** Your examiner will make a final assessment of the Spanish you have used during the test and will award a mark out of 20.

The following pages in this section give you:

- sample tests and tips on what candidates have found helpful. You will find three examples of each type of the three role plays.

- advice and sample questions on the **Presentation, Discussion** and **General Conversation** performed by one Foundation and two Higher Tier candidates (this material is recorded on the cassette).

- answers giving you further tips so that you can achieve your best.

To help you further, there is a transcript of all the role plays and some of the conversation topics (one per candidate) in the Appendix.

ROLE PLAYS

Section 1: Foundation

Card 1

Situation: you are in a café with a friend. Your teacher will play the part of the waiter/waitress and will start the conversation.

You will need to:

- say coffee with milk or another hot drink

- say mineral water or another cold drink

- ask for crisps or something else to eat

- ask for the toilets

Card 2

Situation: You call into a Youth Hostel in Spain. Your teacher will play the part of the hostel worker and will start the conversation.

You will need to:

- ask for beds

- say how many people (e.g. 2 people)

- say for how long (e.g. 1 night)

- ask the price

Card 3

Situation: You are in a post office. Your teacher will play the part of the shopkeeper and will start the conversation.

You will need to:

- say postcards or another item of stationery

- say 2 stamps or something else you would find in a post office

- say for France or another European country

- ask the price

Section 2: Common Exercises

Card 1

Situation: You work in a restaurant at the weekend. You are talking to your Spanish friend about your job. You mention what time you start and what you do. Your teacher will play the part of the Spanish friend and will start the conversation.

You will need to:

- mention the time you start

- say two things about the restaurant

- say what you do

- answer a question

Card 2

Situation: While driving with your family in Spain, you have an accident. You are on the N-110 road near Navafría. You telephone the emergency services. Your teacher will play the part of the garage worker and will start the conversation.

You will need to:

- say who you are and why you are calling

- give the make and colour of your vehicle

- say that one person is injured

- answer the question

Card 3

Situation: Your Spanish friend has just arrived to stay for a few days. You tell him/her that his/her room is upstairs. Ask what he/she likes to eat and if he/she wants to go to the disco tonight. Your teacher will play the part of the Spanish friend and will start the conversation.

You will need to:

- tell your friend where his/her room is (e.g. upstairs)

- ask what he/she likes to eat

- ask if he/she wants to go to the disco

- answer a question

Section 3: Higher

Card 1

Situation: The notes and pictures below give an outline of events during a work experience placement in Spain last summer. Tell the examiner what happened. You need not mention every detail but you must cover the main events.

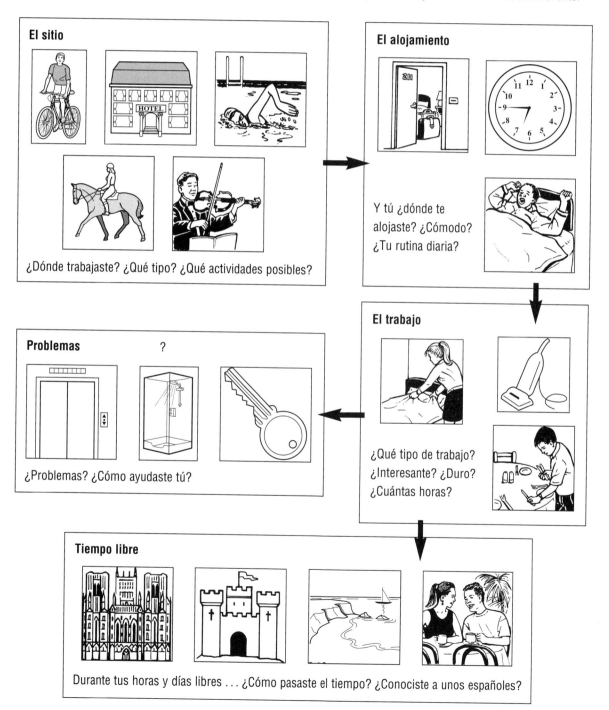

El sitio

¿Dónde trabajaste? ¿Qué tipo? ¿Qué actividades posibles?

El alojamiento

Y tú ¿dónde te alojaste? ¿Cómodo? ¿Tu rutina diaria?

El trabajo

¿Qué tipo de trabajo? ¿Interesante? ¿Duro? ¿Cuántas horas?

Problemas   ?

¿Problemas? ¿Cómo ayudaste tú?

Tiempo libre

Durante tus horas y días libres ... ¿Cómo pasaste el tiempo? ¿Conociste a unos españoles?

Card 2

Situation: The notes and pictures below give an outline of events during an exchange visit to Spain last year. Tell the examiner what happened. You need not mention every detail but you must cover the main events.

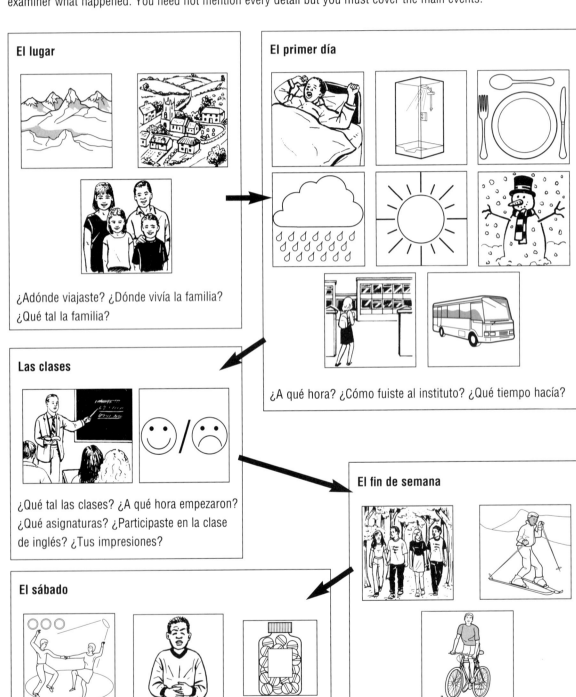

El lugar

¿Adónde viajaste? ¿Dónde vivía la familia?
¿Qué tal la familia?

El primer día

¿A qué hora? ¿Cómo fuiste al instituto? ¿Qué tiempo hacía?

Las clases

¿Qué tal las clases? ¿A qué hora empezaron?
¿Qué asignaturas? ¿Participaste en la clase
de inglés? ¿Tus impresiones?

El fin de semana

¿Qué actividades?

El sábado

¿Una fiesta? Y después, ¿enfermo/a? ¿Quién?

Card 3

Situation: The notes and pictures below give an outline of birthday celebrations last year. Tell the examiner what happened. You need not mention every detail but you must cover the main events.

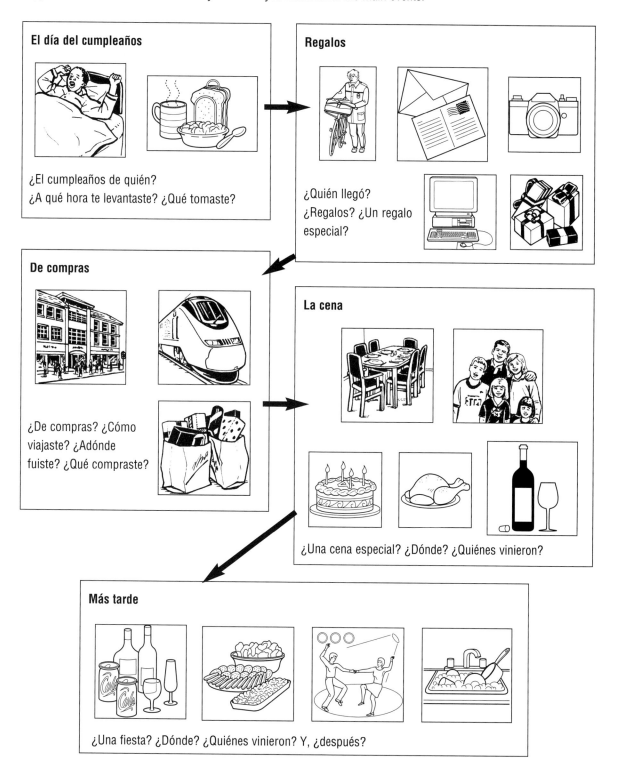

El día del cumpleaños

¿El cumpleaños de quién?
¿A qué hora te levantaste? ¿Qué tomaste?

Regalos

¿Quién llegó?
¿Regalos? ¿Un regalo especial?

De compras

¿De compras? ¿Cómo viajaste? ¿Adónde fuiste? ¿Qué compraste?

La cena

¿Una cena especial? ¿Dónde? ¿Quiénes vinieron?

Más tarde

¿Una fiesta? ¿Dónde? ¿Quiénes vinieron? Y, ¿después?

PRESENTATION, DISCUSSION AND GENERAL CONVERSATION

Candidate 1 – Foundation Tier

Presentation and Discussion – *Mi Pasatiempo Favorito*

At both Foundation and Higher Tier, you need to aim to talk for about one minute and to present all your main points in a clear, straightforward way. You need to give opinions (such as likes and dislikes) and give explanations of your opinions.

HOW TO PREPARE A PRESENTATION

■ Prepare a cue card on a topic on which you feel confident e.g.:

Mi familia – ¿cuántas personas?
Mi madre – descripción
Mi padre – descripción
Mi hermana y mi hermano

■ Stick to your cue card – don't try to do something different on the day of the test.

■ Practise your 1 minute delivery and time yourself.

■ Record yourself and try to make it sound interesting!

■ Give a factual account and add some opinions such as these:

Positive Ideas	Negative Ideas
Me gusta	*No me gusta*
Me encanta	*Odio*
Es fenomenal	*Es desagradable*
Es maravilloso	*Es espantoso*
Es divertido	*No es divertido*
Es interesante	*No es interesante*
Es agradable	*No es agradable*

■ Link short sentences together and use *porque* to explain opinions.

■ Remember that you can use photos, diagrams etc. if you want to illustrate your talk.

DISCUSSION OF THE PRESENTATION

■ Before the test day, think of the kind of questions linked to this topic that you might be asked.

■ Remember that your examiner will spend $1^1/_2$ to 2 minutes questioning you and discussing your material further, so be ready to talk about things linked to the topic such as yourself, family routine, what you do together etc.

■ Your presentation will be marked out of 4. The discussion part of your presentation will be assessed alongside the two general conversation topics.

General Conversation: Topic 1 – School; Topic 2 – Local Area

The candidate you hear on the cassette talks about his school and his local area. Express an opinion simply and clearly wherever possible. The General Conversation is marked out of 10 for communication.

You will not be awarded a linguistic quality mark for the conversation section alone. Your teacher will consider your **whole** performance across the test. It is important, though, to have some precise goals in the General Conversation section so as to score well in the final overall linguistic quality assessment. These goals are:

■ Learn phrases for **all seven topics** in different tenses, past, present and future.

■ Learn vocabulary carefully and try to sound Spanish!

Here are some of the questions on the two topics given to Candidate 1. Use these to help you prepare.

SCHOOL
1. *¿Eres alumno/a en qué tipo de instituto? ¿Cuántos alumnos hay?*
2. *Describe tu instituto.*
3. *¿Las clases empiezan y terminan a qué hora?*
4. *¿Cuáles son tus asignaturas favoritas? ¿Por qué?*
5. *¿Llevas uniforme? Describe tu uniforme. ¿Cuál es tu opinión de tu uniforme?*
6. *¿Qué haces durante la hora de comer?*
7. *¿Practicas deportes en tu instituto? ¿Te gusta?*
8. *¿Eres miembro de un club o de un equipo en tu instituto?*
9. *Describe lo que hiciste ayer en tu instituto.*
10. *Describe lo que vas a hacer después de los exámenes. ¿Vas a seguir con tus estudios?*

LOCAL AREA
1. *¿Dónde vives exactamente?*
2. *¿Desde hace cuántos años vives allí?*
3. *¿Cómo es tu barrio/tu pueblo/tu ciudad?*
4. *¿Cuántos habitantes hay en tu pueblo/tu ciudad?*
5. *¿Qué se puede hacer para divertirse?*
6. *Si vas de compras ¿dónde vas? ¿Cómo vas? ¿Hay autobuses?*
7. *Si quieres ir al supermercado ¿dónde vas? ¿Está lejos? ¿Te gusta ir al supermercado?*
8. *Describe lo que hiciste cuando saliste por última vez.*
9. *¿Te gusta tu región? ¿Por qué? ¿Por qué no?*
10. *En tu ciudad/región ¿qué te gustaría cambiar?*

Now listen to the candidate on the cassette and try answering the questions yourself.

Candidate 2 – Higher Tier

Presentation and Discussion – *Mi Intercambio*

At the Higher Tier you need to aim to go beyond presenting factual information. You should try to express opinions and say **why** you have these opinions.

HOW TO PREPARE A PRESENTATION AT HIGHER TIER

- Prepare a cue card, e.g.

  Mi intercambio – ¿cuándo? ¿con quién? ¿el viaje?

  Madrid y la Sierra Nevada

  El camping en Granada – ¿tus impresiones?

  Aspectos positivos de mi estancia

Stick to the cue card and practise delivering your presentation in a confident and lively way. It needs to sound as **natural** as possible. Use emphasis and intonation to make it more interesting.

- Record yourself and try to identify errors of pronunciation and intonation upon which you can improve.

- Try to include some of the following structures which will improve your style:
  - *al* followed by the infinitive (e.g. *al llegar a Madrid*)
  - *después de haber* followed by a past participle (e.g. *después de haber pasado dos semanas en Madrid*)
  - *para* followed by an infinitive (e.g. *para ir de compras*)

- Use **a variety of tenses** (perfect, preterite, present, future, imperfect, conditional).

- Try not to use just *yo* (the first person).

- Give **opinions and reasons**, using introductory phrases such as *Creo que era . . . me gustó la experiencia porque . . . sobre todo me gustaba . . . lo que me gustaba más era*

- Use **conjunctions** such as *pero*, *porque* and **adverbs of time** such as *luego, más tarde, después* to add variety.

- Make sure you can express how you **feel** about something e.g. *Estaba satisfecho(a)/no estaba satisfecho(a)*, adding a reason or reasons wherever possible.

DISCUSSION OF THE PRESENTATION

- Think of the content of what you have presented and imagine the kinds of questions which could be asked.

- Listen carefully to the questions and be sure you have understood the **tense** so that you can answer in the correct tense.

- The discussion will follow on from the presentation and will be marked for communication together with the two conversation topics.

- The overall linguistic quality mark will take into account the language you use in the discussion and conversation.

- Be daring, give your opinions and be enthusiastic!

General Conversation: Topic 1 – Career, Work, Work Experience; Topic 2 – School

The candidate you will hear (Candidate 2) talks about the above two topics. At Higher Tier you should be prepared to talk about both topics at equal length, giving your opinions and reasons for these opinions as naturally as possible. Your examiner may put a point of view to you, so be prepared to agree or disagree when asked what you think.

■ **Phrases for agreement**
Estoy de acuerdo contigo
¡Por supuesto!
¡Claro!
Sí, tienes razón

■ **Phrases for when you want to say "perhaps ... but"**
Sí, tienes razón, quizás, pero yo creo que ...
Es posible/probable pero en mi opinión ...
Es verdad pero/sin embargo ...

■ **Phrases for disagreement**
No. No estoy de acuerdo
No, muy al contrario
No te creo

■ **Phrases to give you time to think!**
No sé. Es un punto de vista interesante pero yo creo que ...
Es una cuestón bastante difícil pero en mi opinión ...
Vamos ... pienso que ...

Here are some questions on the two topics given to Candidate 2. Use these to help you prepare.

CAREER, WORK, WORK EXPERIENCE
1. *¿Tienes un empleo? ¿Dónde trabajas?*
2. *¿Cuántas horas trabajas a la semana?*
3. *¿Qué opinas de tu trabajo?*
4. *¿Tienes experiencia de trabajo? ¿Qué has hecho exactamente?*
5. *¿Cuál es tu opinión de tu trabajo? ¿Era útil?*
6. *¿Qué aprendiste?*
7. *¿En qué quieres trabajar en el futuro?*
8. *¿Por qué has escogido este trabajo?*
9. *¿Qué vas a hacer el año que viene?*
10. *¿Vas a seguir con tus estudios? ¿Por qué/Por qué no?*

SCHOOL
1. *Describe tu instituto – los edificios, el número de alumnos etc.*
2. *¿Qué asignaturas has escogido y por qué?*
3. *¿Cómo son los profesores en tu instituto? ¿Hay buenas relaciones entre los profesores y los alumnos?*
4. *¿Llevas uniforme? ¿Qué opinas?*
5. *¿Cuáles son las ventajas y las desventajas de un uniforme?*
6. *Describe lo que hiciste en tu instituto ayer.*
7. *¿Qué cosas te gustaría cambiar? ¿Por qué?*

8. *¿Qué vas a hacer después de tus exámenes?*

9. *¿Cuáles son tus ambiciones?*

10. *¿Tus años en el instituto te han preparado bien para la vida? ¿Por qué/Por qué no?*

Now listen to the candidate on the cassette and try answering the questions yourself.

Candidate 3 – Higher Tier

Presentation and Discussion: *Mi Experiencia Del Trabajo*

All the comments made above about the Presentation for Candidates 1 and 2 are equally relevant here. You are again aiming to give a good introductory talk which will lead naturally into a discussion. Re-read the notes on how to prepare a Presentation at Higher Tier.

PREPARING THE CUE CARD

You may find it useful to use symbols such as + (positive opinions) and − (negative opinions) on your card. Never use English words on it. Simple diagrams and spider webs can be useful. Here is an example of a cue card for *Mi experiencia del trabajo*:

At the preparation stage you could use more Spanish phrases on the card and gradually reduce it to the main titles above. Remember that you can use photos, leaflets or objects as part of your presentation if you wish.

DISCUSSION OF THE PRESENTATION

■ Re-read the guidance tips for Candidates 1 and 2 and memorise the phrases for agreement and disagreement.

■ Remember to think of the questions you are likely to be asked. Make a list of them and look up and learn any vocabulary or expressions you might need.

■ Revise preterite and imperfect tenses carefully as you will need them in the discussion.

General Conversation: Topic 1 – Free Time; Topic 2 – Holidays

In this section, remember the importance of using a variety of tenses, structures and opinions. Do not always wait for the examiner to ask you another question – try and add something to your last answer. You can steer the conversation too, provided that you don't stray too far off the subject!

FREE TIME

1. *¿Qué haces normalmente cuando estás libre por la tarde/durante el fin de semana?*

2. *Habla de tu pasatiempo favorito. ¿Lo haces desde cuándo?*

3. *¿Te gustan los deportes? ¿Por qué/Por qué no?*

4. *¿Cuántas horas al día ves la tele?*

5. *¿Qué tipo de programa te gusta? ¿Por qué?*

6. *¿Te gusta la música? ¿Qué clase?*

7. *¿Tocas un instrumento musical?*

8. *Habla de lo que hiciste el fin de semana pasado.*

9. *¿Cuáles son tus planes para el fin de semana que viene?*

10. *Si tuvieras mucho dinero, ¿qué deporte o actividad te gustaría practicar?*

HOLIDAYS

1. *¿Dónde prefieres pasar tus vacaciones y con quién?*

2. *¿Cómo prefieres viajar y por qué?*

3. *¿Dónde fuiste de vacaciones el año pasado?*

4. *Habla de tus vacaciones del año pasado. ¿Dónde te quedaste? ¿Con quién? ¿Qué hiciste?*

5. *¿La vida en ... es muy distinta de la vida en Gran Bretaña?*

6. *¿Cómo era la comida en ... ?*

7. *¿Qué te gustaba más en ... ?*

8. *¿Quieres volver? ¿Por qué?*

9. *¿Tienes planes para el verano que viene? ¿Adónde irás?*

10. *Describe tus vacaciones ideales.*

ANSWERS AND TIPS

Note: the answers and tips which follow refer to the three candidates you hear on the cassette.

Role Plays

Section 1: Foundation

Tips

Remember that answers do **not** have to be long but must communicate the main message. When you read the instructions, remember the following:

"Ask for" = ***Quiero ...***

"Ask if they have" = ***¿Tienen ...?***

"Ask where" = ***¿Dónde está(n) ... ?***

"Is there"/"Are there ... ?" = ***¿Hay ... ?***

"Ask when/at what time" = ***¿A qué hora?***

Frequently tested topics are **arranging to go out; shopping; café/restaurant; buying tickets; transport; hotel/camp site**. Revise carefully numbers 1–100, quantities (e.g. weights) and the above phrases.

The number in brackets (2) below refers to the number of marks for each successfully communicated response.

Suggested Responses

CARD 1

– *Un café con leche, por favor.*	(2)
– *Agua mineral, por favor.*	(2)
– *Patatas, por favor.*	(2)
– *¿Dónde están los servicios?*	(2)

 Tips   Make sure you know how to order things in a café – coffee, tea, sandwiches (e.g. cheese and ham) – and how to ask for the bill.

CARD 2

– *¿Hay camas?*	(2)
– *Somos dos.*	(2)
– *Una noche.*	(2)
– *¿Cuánto cuesta?*	(2)

 Tips   Be sure to know how to book accommodation. The different types of rooms, singles, doubles and facilities (such as the dining room, the lift, shower, bathroom etc.) are commonly tested.

CARD 3

– *Postales, por favor.*	(2)
– *Y quiero dos sellos, por favor.*	(2)
– *Para Francia.*	(2)
– *¿Cuánto es?*	(2)

 Tips   The answers could be shorter. You don't have to use *quiero* or *por favor* but it sounds better and politer to include them. Remember to learn numbers 1–100 very carefully!

Section 2: Common Exercises

Communicating the message is still important, obviously, but you need to be as accurate as you can, especially when you have to produce a longer message which contains a verb. You also need to be able to use tenses other than the present. While preparing, think of what the examiner may say as the lead-in to *Answer a question*. Listen to the examiner very carefully and ask him/her to repeat if you haven't understood.

CARD 1

– *Empiezo a las nueve.* (2)

– *El restaurante es moderno y cómodo.* (2)

– *Lavo los platos/sirvo las comidas.* (2)

– *Cuarenta libras.* (2)

> **Tips**   The / indicates alternative answers. You can give any time for Task 1. For the last task do not be confused between *cuánto* (how much) and *cuándo* (when).

CARD 2

– *Me llamo Sam Jones. Hemos tenido un accidente.* (2)

– *Es un Fiat rojo.* (2)

– *Una persona está herida.* (2)

– *Es mi hermano.* (2)

> **Tips**   You need to know that *herir* means to wound or to injure, *una herida* is an injury and *un(a) herido(a)* is an injured person

CARD 3

– *Tu habitación está arriba.*

– *¿Qué te gusta comer?*

– *¿Quieres ir a la discoteca?*

– *A las once.*

> **Tips**   Make sure you know that *arriba* is upstairs and *abajo* is downstairs

Section 3: Higher

> **Tips**   This kind of role play always requires you to give details of travelling, leisure activities and eating and drinking. Learn the essentials such as how you travelled, phrases for starting, breaking and finishing a journey, how you spent your free time and what you bought for a picnic or ordered in a restaurant.

CANDIDATE 1

The candidate scores 8 out of a possible 8 for communication.

The candidate communicates all of the main points and does not rely on the examiner to get through the story. When the examiner intervenes, the candidate is able to understand the interventions and reply appropriately. The candidate is able to offer imagined detail, express and justify opinions and maintains a good pace. Fluency is maintained throughout. In assessing the linguistic accuracy, the examiner would bear in mind here that the use of preterite and imperfect tenses was correct and the intonation and pronunciation were generally accurate.

CANDIDATE 2

This is a very solid performance. All the main points are communicated and no guidance is needed from the examiner. The candidate can give reasons or justifications for his opinions and is quite fluent. There are few hesitations and the pace is quite brisk. However there was a lack of detail: the role play was rather short so a mark of 6 is awarded. Linguistic quality would be marked at the end of the whole test, but worthy of note here are the very good use of tenses, vocabulary and structures.

CANDIDATE 3

The candidate communicates all the main points and adds some imaginative detail. The interventions by the examiner are dealt with easily. Opinions are given and justified. However the role play is over too quickly: there is scope for more imaginative detail. The candidate scores 7 out of 8 for communication.

Now look at the transcript for these role plays and then try them yourself using the candidate instructions.

Presentation/Discussion/General Conversation

Candidate 1

PRESENTATION

This candidate gives a straightforward factual account of his favourite sport. He has prepared his material well – he can describe accurately and his meaning is clear. He can also express opinions and sometimes he can give explanations of these opinions. He is therefore awarded 4 marks.

DISCUSSION AND GENERAL CONVERSATION

He goes on to discuss his presentation and can not only answer the questions with ease, he can also add material and develop the conversation. The candidate's message is clear and opinions are expressed. He moves on to answer questions about school and his local area. Both topics are dealt with comprehensively. The messages are clear, tense use is accurate, opinions are expressed and justified and grammar is correct. Full marks (10) are scored.

Tips   Study the questions asked and work through the answers. Think carefully about "time markers", i.e. words such as *ayer* and *el año pasado*, these should signal to you the need to talk in the past. If you hear *quieres* in the question you are being asked about what you would like to do. If you hear *generalmente* or *normalmente*, use the present tense.

Candidate 2

PRESENTATION

The candidate gives a lively and well organised presentation. She communicates all points clearly and as she can also express a range of opinions, giving reasons where necessary, she scores 4 marks.

DISCUSSION AND GENERAL CONVERSATION

The discussion shows that the candidate is able to talk freely about her subject. The examiner has little need to rephrase questions and the candidate is able to give a good range of opinions and can justify them.

She covers both conversation topics (Career/work/work experience and School Life) well. She does not always wait for a question to be asked – she is quite prepared to develop her own part in the conversation without being invited to join in by the examiner. She appears confident and can take the initiative in conversation. This performance is worthy of 10 out of 10 for communication.

Candidate 3

PRESENTATION

The candidate talks about his work experience in a hotel. He has prepared his presentation very well. He does not rush, but delivers his material in a fluent and clear way. He expresses his opinions readily and can always back these up with further explanations. He would score the full 4 marks.

DISCUSSION AND GENERAL CONVERSATION

He goes on to discuss his presentation in a mature way, maintaining his high standard of Spanish. He talks freely and naturally.

He then discusses the topics of free time and holidays. He impresses with the ease with which he responds to the questions. He goes well beyond the factual and expresses a wide range of opinions. This is an outstanding performance worthy of 10 marks for communication.
In assessing the linguistic quality of this candidate, there are several excellent qualities to note. He can move from tense to tense, always using them appropriately and accurately. He is able to compare and contrast his experiences, using appropriate language, and he includes good structures such as "dependent infinitives' (i.e. two verbs together, with the second in the infinitive). His pronunciation and intonation and his overall accuracy are excellent, certainly worthy of the top mark for linguistic quality!

5 – Writing

General Hints

Writing is in many ways the most difficult of the language skills. It is the last skill we acquire when learning our mother tongue, we take a long time to learn the spelling and grammar of a foreign language and, in answering exam questions, there is no scope for making inspired guesses as can sometimes be the case for listening and reading.

Your ability to write in Spanish is dependent on your familiarity with the language so that the more fluent you become in speaking and the greater practice you have in listening to the language the easier you will find it to express yourself in writing.

At Foundation Tier writing, accuracy is important, but the most essential aspect is **communication** or the ability to make yourself understood. That means that spelling mistakes, errors with verb endings and so on can be tolerated as long as they don't make your message unclear. It would be unreasonable to expect you to write fully correct Spanish, as most of us make mistakes when writing English.

In the Common section and particularly on the Higher Tier, however, those who write stylish, accurate Spanish obviously deserve to be rewarded. You will acquire a good grade if you can write comprehensible Spanish, but you will only reach the top grades if you can show in addition that you have a good range of vocabulary and style and that you understand and can use the principles of Spanish grammar.

For the writing skill you may be entered for the final exam or you may be doing coursework. The examples on the following pages, however, are of examination exercises. There is a separate section of advice on coursework on page 77.

Here are some points to bear in mind when doing your writing exam:

- **Watch the time.** On Foundation Tier you will have four exercises, each one more demanding and therefore requiring more time. Pace yourself carefully so that you have enough time to give a good answer for the final question – the letter of 100 words. On Higher Tier you have only two exercises, but the second has to be longer and is more demanding than the first, so again divide your time accordingly.

- **Read the questions carefully.** Be sure that you know what you have to do. Study any examples provided. Where a number of points must be included (in the letter, for example) make sure you have addressed each by ticking them off as you deal with them. You will only gain high marks if you deal with **all** the points.

- **Write enough words.** 90–100 words are expected on the letter and 140–150 on the article or report. Although you should not spend too long counting your words, you need to check that you have written enough. It is far more important, however, to ensure that you have dealt with **all** the points.

- **Verbs!** You must be able to show that you can handle verbs in Spanish. In Common and Higher questions, only accurate verb structures will gain you the highest marks. It is particularly important to be confident in the writing of verbs in different tenses; in both the Common and the Higher papers, your ability to use the preterite tense (e.g. *trabajé/fui*) and the future tense (e.g. *saldré/voy a salir*) **must** be shown in order to acquire a good grade. You should also show that you are able to use other tenses such as the imperfect and also the conditional. Refer to the grammar section (page 79) and be sure to learn the rules for tense formation. Remember, too, to learn other parts of verbs as well as the first person (*yo*).

- **Opinions!** As in speaking, in order to gain a grade C or above, you must show your ability to express opinions. Learn phrases that can introduce opinions, e.g. *en mi opinión*, *creo que*, *pienso que*; and also in the past tense, e.g. *mi opinión era que*; *creía que*. Learn also how to give **reasons**, e.g. *me gusta mi dormitorio porque es cómodo*.

- **Develop a style.** Learn some good phrases and try to use them in the Common and Higher questions, though only if it is appropriate to include them. Try to link sentences by using phrases such as *Después de haber terminado mi trabajo....* or *Antes de salir de la casa....* Try to vary your language so that, for instance, you don't always use *mucho* to express the idea of "a lot" – learn and use phrases such as *una gran cantidad de....*

- **Be as accurate as you can.** Despite what is written above about errors not automatically resulting in low marks, it is obvious that the more accurate you can be the better the reward. Be particularly careful to check verb endings and adjective forms (e.g. *una pequeña habitación*, *son jóvenes*). Show that **you** are able to avoid the spelling errors that so many other candidates make, by being sure of the difference between *caballo* and *cabello*, *ciudad* and *cuidado*, *mes* and *mesa* etc.

- **Check your work.** After you have finished your letter, list or article, check it. First check that you have included all the details asked for. Then read it through closely, checking for accuracy, and paying particular attention to verb forms such as endings. If you have written in the past tense, do you know which verbs are regular and which verbs are irregular? Use all your available time at the end of the exam looking for mistakes.

- **Don't write your answers in rough first.** By all means do a quick plan, but don't waste time copying up a rough version at the end of the exam. It is easy to make errors when copying and you wouldn't have time to do this anyway.

Section 1: Foundation

The opening exercise is a simple list-writing task requiring either eight different items or, in this case, four items with a description.

Exercise 1

Write a list **in Spanish** of four things in the lounge with a description.

Ejemplo	*una lámpara*	*amarilla*
Ejemplo	*un piano*	*viejo*
1		
2		
3		
4		

[Total : 8 marks]

In this next Foundation exercise you have to write short sentences.

Exercise 2

Write about 40 words in Spanish about your work.

Example:

¿dónde trabajas?

Trabajo en un supermercado.

---

*   ¿qué día trabajas?

*   ¿las horas?

*   ¿cuánto te pagan?

*   ¿cómo vas al trabajo?

*   ¿tu opinión?

Notas sobre mi trabajo

*

*

*

*

*

*

[Total : 10 marks]

For the third exercise you will have more opportunity to write longer sentences.

Exercise 3

Write an e-mail to your friend.
Give a description in Spanish of yourself, your family and school.

Write about 40 words in complete sentences.

Example: ■ where you live

Vivo en Manchester

Mention the following:

■ your brother or sister or pet
■ your house
■ your personality
■ your hobbies
■ your school

Section 2: Common Exercises

For these exercises, common to both Foundation and Higher Tiers, accuracy becomes more important and you need to be able to show that you can use a range of tenses. The instructions are now given in Spanish. You will have a choice of question. You can be sure that the tasks will require you to write in the past, present and future and you will have to give at least one opinion.

Ejercicio 4

Escribe una carta 90–100 palabras **en español** sobre tu instituto.
Menciona :

- desde hace cuánto tiempo estás en este instituto
- una descripción del instituto (el edificio, el uniforme, un día típico)
- la asignatura que te gusta más y por qué
- un viaje escolar que hiciste
- lo que vas a hacer cuando dejes el instituto

Ejercicio 5

Vas a visitar a tu amigo en Madrid.
Escribe una carta de 90–100 palabras **en español**.
Menciona:

- cómo vas a viajar
- dos cosas que quieres hacer en Madrid
- tus razones
- algo que hiciste el año pasado
- haz una pregunta sobre Madrid

Ejercicio 6

Escribe 90–100 palabras **en español** sobre tu trabajo y tu dinero de bolsillo.
Menciona:

- cuánto dinero recibes
- lo que compraste recientemente
- lo que haces para ayudar en casa
- lo que haces los fines de semana
- el trabajo que vas a hacer en el futuro

Section 3: Higher

These are the most demanding exercises, for which you have to write about 150 words and in which you must display your ability to write correct Spanish with a certain style. In addition to the features required for grade C (tenses, opinions), you must also be able to use longer sequences and use a wide range of vocabulary structure and tense. You must be able to narrate events and express and justify points of view. You are given a choice of question. Although four examples are given here, in the exam there will only be a choice of two.

Ejercicio 7

Escribe un reportaje de 140–150 palabras **en español** sobre tus vacaciones en el extranjero.
Menciona:

- dónde fuiste
- tus impresiones del país
- si prefieres vacaciones en Gran Bretaña o en el extranjero
- da razones

Ejercicio 8

Escribe un reportaje de 140–150 palabras **en español** sobre una semana de trabajo (por ejemplo en una oficina, en una fábrica, en una tienda).
Menciona:

- las horas que trabajaste
- dinero
- tus colegas
- lo que hiciste
- tus impresiones (¿buenas o malas? ¿por qué)
- lo que vas a hacer en el futuro y explica por qué

Ejercicio 9

Buscas un trabajo en España durante las vacaciones de verano.
Escribe una carta de 140–150 palabras **en español** contestando a un anuncio.
Menciona:

- las fechas posibles
- trabajo que ya has hecho
- tus talentos
- por qué tus talentos son especiales

Ejercicio 10

¿Estás en buena condición física? ¿Te gusta la vida? ¿Quieres contribuir a nuestro debate?

Tu dieta.   Tus actividades deportivas.   ¿Es importante estar en buena condición? ¿Por qué?

Escribe un artículo de 140–150 palabras **en español** contribuyendo al debate.

SAMPLE ANSWERS AND TIPS

Section 1

Exercise 1

Sample answer

perro perezoso, sofá cómodo, flores bonitas, mesa verde, ordenador nuevo

> **Tips**
> In this exercise, look at the example first. It tells you what you have to do. This opening exercise is designed to be simple, to give you confidence at the start of the exam but you must aim to gain the full eight marks in order to give yourself a better chance of scoring enough marks overall to reach Grade C standard. The picture is provided to give examples of the items to include, but you are free to write others as long as they are relevant to the task set. Write the ones that you are sure of first. Although you must of course avoid writing in English, you may use words such as *piano* which are the same in both English and Spanish.

Exercise 2

Sample answer

Trabajo los sábados y los domingos desde las siete de la mañana hasta las tres de la tarde. Me pagan 5 libras a la hora. Voy al trabajo andando. En mi opinión el trabajo es agradable.

> **Tips**
> There is no need to rewrite the example. Take each point in turn and deal with it simply and as correctly as you can. Note that you can answer points 1 and 2 in a single sentence, but try to use as many correct verbs as you can.

Exercise 3

Sample answer

Hola. Me llamo Paula. Tengo una hermana pero no tengo hermanos. Mi casa es bonita y está en el centro de la ciudad. Soy una persona alegre y generosa. Me gusta nadar y salir. Mi instituto es moderno pero no me gusta.

> **Tips**
> There is no need to include the example. Take each point in turn and deal with it simply and as correctly as you can. At this stage of the exam the examiner is not looking for elegant Spanish.

Section 2

Ejercicio 4

Sample answer

Hola Natalia. Voy a escribir de mi instituto. Se llama London High School y estudio aquí desde hace cuatro años. Es bastante moderno pero es demasiado grande. Hay novecientos alumnos y cincuenta profesores. La asignatura que me gusta más es el español, ¡claro! Es interesante y el profesor es joven y muy guapo.

El año pasado el profesor de español organizó un intercambio con un instituto en Granada. Viajamos en avión y lo pasamos muy bien. Visité los sitios de interés y compré ropa española. El año que viene, voy a dejar el instituto y estudiaré el español en un colegio.

Tips

Now that you have completed the Foundation exercises, you have to show that you can write opinions and use different tenses. Did you notice the different tenses required in Task 4 (past) and Task 5 (future)? Note the useful opening phrase *voy a escribir de* . . . . In Task 1, the present tense is used with *desde hace* to say you have been doing something **and still are**. Learn the phrase *aprendo el español desde hace cinco años* as an example of this.

This answer contains 97 words. When counting words, don't count English words or names such as the name of your school.

It is worth giving as many examples as you can of past and future tenses.

Be wary of the word *hay* (there is/there are). If you have to use it, use it once only. Overuse of *hay* tells the examiner you cannot use verbs. If you are asked for an opinion, give one even if it is only *me gusta*. . . .

Ejercicio 5

Sample answer

Birmingham, 5 de marzo

Hola, Miguel
¿Qué tal? Voy a escribirte de mi visita a Madrid. Voy a tomar el avión desde aquí el seis de agosto y voy a llegar a eso de las ocho de la noche.

Durante mi visita me gustaría ver el museo del Prado porque me gusta la pintura. También quisiera conocer a tus amigos para poder practicar mi español. El año pasado pasé dos semanas en la Costa Brava con mi familia. Desafortunadamente no podía hablar en español porque todo el mundo era inglés.

¿Hay un club de fútbol en Madrid? ¿Puedo ver un partido de fútbol?

Hasta pronto
Andrew

Tips

Note that you have to mention **two** activities, with a reason for each. Since the visit is still to come you need to use the future tense (e.g. *voy a tomar*) but you could use the other form of the future (e.g. *tomaré*). The **preterite** tense is required in Task 4. Note that you must ask a question at the end. Don't forget also the phrase *¿Puedo . . .?* which means "can I?" Remember that, for variation, you can use the phrase *quisiera*, which means the same as *quiero*. When saying you will arrive **on** a particular date you don't need any word to translate "on". As this is a letter, don't forget to write a suitable beginning and end.

Ejercicio 6

Sample answer

Oxford, 15 de mayo.

Querido amigo:

¿Qué tal? Voy a escribir del dinero que recibo. Como dinero de bolsillo recibo diez libras a la semana de mis padres. No es mucho. Compré muchas cosas el sábado pasado. Fui al centro de la ciudad y compré una camisa, una corbata y un CD. Por la tarde comí en McDonald's. Era caro. Para ganar dinero ayudo a mis padres en casa. Por ejemplo hago mi cama y arreglo mi dormitorio todos los días. Los sábados lavo el coche de mi madre y de vez en cuando hago la jardinería. En el futuro voy a trabajar como mecánico y voy a ganar mucho dinero. ¡Espero que sí!

Saludos
David

 Tips
> Although we've mentioned how important it is to be able to use the past and future tenses, you mustn't forget how to use the present! Note the examples in Tasks 1, 3 and 4 here. Note the effective use of phrases like *era caro* (it cost a lot), *de vez en cuando* (from time to time), *no es mucho* (it's not a lot) and *espero que sí* (I hope so!)

Section 3

Ejercicio 7

Sample answer

El año pasado pasé unas vacaciones magníficas en Italia. Fui allí con un grupo de mi instituto. El profesor de historia organizó el viaje porque habíamos estudiado la historia romana durante el año. Las ruinas antiguas eran inolvidables. Visitamos el Coliseo, todos los monumentos y la parte vieja de la ciudad. Sin embargo no podía ver todo, así que tengo ganas de volver un día. Lo que me gustaba en Roma era la arquitectura. Lo que no me gustaba era el tráfico – hay tantos coches y andan tan deprisa. A pesar de mis recuerdos agradables, creo que prefiero pasar mis vacaciones en Gran Bretaña. No hablo bien las lenguas extranjeras y nosotros tenemos unas ruinas maravillosas en Inglaterra. Además prefiero la comida inglesa – no me gustan los espaguetis. Pero mis amigos dicen que volverán a Italia el año que viene.

 Tips
> This answer would earn a very good mark because it is very accurate. There is a good range of tenses (including preterite, present and future), reasons have been given and justified and there is style in the writing. Equally importantly, all the points mentioned in the question have been dealt with. You should make a brief plan before starting an essay of this type to ensure that you have covered all that is asked for. You will always be asked to give your reactions, opinions or impressions and you should be confident in using the appropriate phrases. Some of the good points in this essay and which you should note are:
>
> ■ adjective agreement, e.g. *unas vacaciones magnífic**as**; la parte vie**ja**; las lenguas extranjer**as***
> ■ use of past, present and future tenses and also the use of the **pluperfect tense** – *habíamos estudiado* (we **had** studied)
> ■ stylish vocabulary, e.g. *inolvidable* (unforgettable).
> ■ the use of phrases such as *Lo que me gustaba*, *Lo que no me gustaba*
> ■ words such as *a pesar de* (despite), *sin embargo* (however), *además* (moreover)

Ejercicio 8

Sample answer

En marzo del año pasado, pasé una semana trabajando en un supermercado en mi ciudad. Todos los días tenía que empezar a las ocho y trabajaba hasta las cinco con una pausa de una hora para comer. Solía comer a las doce y media. Desafortunadamente no gané ni una peseta porque lo que hacía era [para tener] experiencia de trabajo. Todos los otros empleados del supermercado eran simpáticos y acogedores salvo una mujer que se burlaba de mí. Yo tenía que poner la comida en los estantes lo que era monótono y también trabajar en la caja lo que era más interesante porque podía charlar con los clientes. Por tanto tengo impresiones mixtas de mi trabajo aunque sólo duró una semana. No me gustaría trabajar en el supermercado en el futuro. Lo que me gustaría hacer es trabajar en una escuela primaria porque me encantan los niños. Sí, un día seré maestro.

Tips

Although a little lacking in style, this report is very accurate, covers all the points and contains past, present and future tenses, some good vocabulary and instructions. It would therefore earn an excellent mark. Note in particular the following points:

- the way in which some sentences have been linked with *porque* and *lo que*, making "subordinate clauses" which give better style – e.g. *porque me encantan los niños*, *una mujer que se burlaba de mí*
- good vocabulary, e.g.: *acogedor* (welcoming), with the correct plural ending; *salvo* (except); *solía* (I used to . . .); *desafortunadamente* (unfortunately); *no . . . ni una peseta* (not a single peseta); *por tanto* (therefore)
- a mixture of tenses: preterite (*pasé*), imperfect (*trabajaba*), conditional (*me gustaría*), future (*seré*)
- the use of *lo que*, e.g. *lo que era monótono. . .* (which was boring)

Ejercicio 9

Sample answer

Bath, 14 de marzo

Estimado Señor:

He visto su anuncio en el periódico y le escribo porque me gustaría trabajar en su camping durante agosto. Estoy libre del tres al veinticuatro de agosto. Usted busca jóvenes para trabajar con niños organizando juegos, etcétera. Ya he trabajado con niños. He trabajado en un camping en Francia el año pasado. Organicé juegos, concursos, y otras actividades deportivas y culturales.

Creo que esta experiencia me ayudará mucho.

En cuanto a mis talentos, tengo paciencia y soy amistoso. Me entiendo bien con otra gente, sobre todo con niños. Hablo inglés, francés y español. Estos talentos serán útiles en su camping porque podré trabajar con niños de muchas nacionalidades. En mi opinión es muy importante.

En espera de sus noticias
Le saluda atentamente,

Carolyn Jones

Tips

As you are required to write a letter, remember to give a suitable beginning and end (using the correct style of formal ending) and write your name at the end. Writing a letter applying for a job is a fairly common exam task at this level. As before, you must ensure that you cover all the points. Points worthy of note in this example include:

■ good use of verbs in different tenses – there are examples here of the present, the future, the preterite, the perfect and the conditional. Useful examples of each are:
   Present: *le escribo porque* ... (I am writing to you because); *me entiendo bien con* ... (I get on well with); *Usted busca* (You are looking for); *creo que* (I believe that)
   Future: *podré* (I will be able)
   Perfect: *He visto* (I have seen)
   Preterite: *Organicé* (I organised)
■ remember that the verb *poder* (like *tener que* and *querer*) must be followed by the infinitive of a verb
■ learn the phrases *del* ... *al* ... to use with dates (from ... to ...)
■ note the correct adjective agreements: *útiles*; *actividades deportivas y culturales*.
■ note the opinion phrases: *Creo que*, *En mi opinión*

Ejercicio 10

Sample answer

En mi opinión, la salud es la cosa más importante de la vida. Cuánto más sano eres, más aprecias la vida. Es tan importante hacer todo lo posible para evitar enfermedades y mantenerte en buena condición. Yo estoy en buena condición porque tengo cuidado con lo que como. Además, no fumo, no bebo demasiado y hago ejercicio todos los días. Ayer, por ejemplo, fui de paseo en mi bicicleta. Esta tarde, jugaré al tenis. En cuanto a mi dieta, como fruta y verdura frescas todos los días. No como cosas dulces e intento evitar cosas grasientas. No hago muchos deportes pero muchas veces nado en la piscina y monto a caballo de vez en cuando. Siempre me ha gustado jugar al fútbol. Sí, me encanta la vida porque estoy en buena condición física.

Tips

This is a fairly simple answer but it is accurate. On a question like this, there is not as good an opportunity to use a range of tenses. Most verbs here are in the present tense but they are correct. However, a preterite and a future have been used. Opinions are given and they are justified. Note the following:

■ the use of the words *cuánto más* ... *más* ... to translate "the more ... the more". You can use the word *cuánto menos* ... *menos* ... ("the less ... the less") in the same way.
■ the verb *evitar*, a useful verb meaning "to avoid"
■ time phrases: *de vez en cuando*, *muchas veces*, *todos los días* etc. Learn and use them
■ notice *en cuanto a* (as regards)
■ *además* is a useful alternative to *también*

Coursework

Your teacher will set your coursework tasks. You will do several during the course and towards the end you will select three pieces. You will choose your best pieces, obviously but, as your teacher will explain, they must be drawn from three different contexts and different sub-contexts (see page 2). Furthermore, at least one of these pieces must be one that you have done in class under "controlled conditions", with only a dictionary and no kind of notes to help you.

The mark awarded by your teacher for each piece of coursework will depend on its length, its accuracy, its use of tenses, its inclusion of opinions and reasons and so on. The marking of the communication, accuracy and quality of language is similar to that used for the final writing exam. The mark awarded by your teacher may, of course, be altered by the examiners checking the marking of candidates from your centre.

For those pieces not done under controlled conditions, you are allowed to write a first draft. Remember that your teacher is not allowed to indicate the errors on the first draft but can only give general advice as to how it might be improved. When writing your final draft, check the spelling of every word. You are allowed to use a dictionary as well as other reference materials, and your own earlier work, including practice materials. But remember that the coursework must be your own work. You are not permitted to copy passages from a textbook or ask someone else to help you. You are required to sign a declaration that the work has been written by you alone. If you have used reference materials you must state at the end of each piece which materials you consulted.

You may of course word-process your coursework but remember to include accents – find out how to create these on your word processing program.

6 – Spanish Grammar

The grammar points that follow form the basis of requirements for GCSE but it should be understood that it is not an exhaustive list of what can be tested. Space does not allow a complete guide to the grammar required for GCSE.

Grammar and Linguistic Structures

Essentials for achievement: whether you are going to sit Foundation or Higher papers (or a mix of both) you need to know the rules (or short cuts) which make Spanish work. A full list of the grammar requirements can be found on the OCR GCSE Spanish specification website. This chapter, however, aims to give you the "essentials" that you should try to master. The chapter features a **core** of grammar for **all candidates** and **extension** sections which indicate the grammar and structures that you should try to master in order to attempt the higher tier papers with confidence. Those grammar points or structures marked *R* indicate the points which you should be able to understand in Reading and Listening papers – you would not be expected to produce these in speaking and writing, but if you could, so much the better! It is indicated after each grammar point whether the material is for Foundation Tier (CORE) or Higher Tier (EXTENSION).

Definite and indefinite articles – CORE

	Definite article (the)		Indefinite article (a, an, some)	
	masculine	feminine	masculine	feminine
singular	*el*	*la*	*un*	*una*
plural	*los*	*las*	*unos*	*unas*

de + *el*   becomes *del*
a + *el*   becomes *al*
e.g.   *el libro del chico*   the boy's book
   fui al estadio   I went to the stadium

The definite article is used:
when referring to nouns in a general sense:
   el vino es importante en España   wine is important in Spain

in certain expressions when it is not used in English:
   en la cama   in bed   *en el hospital*   in hospital
   en la iglesia   in church   *en la televisión*   on television
   en la cárcel   in prison   *en el colegio*   in school

with the name of a language except when it comes directly after *aprender*, *hablar* or *saber*:
   el español es fácil   Spanish is easy
   hablo español   I speak Spanish

However, the indefinite article is omitted:
when talking directly to the person:

> *Buenos días, señor García*   Good morning, Mr. García

when saying "on Saturday", "on Friday":

> *el sábado*   on Saturday
>
> *el viernes*   on Friday

The indefinite article is omitted:
before occupations and nationality:

> *ella es profesora*   she is a teacher
>
> *él es inglés*   he is an Englishman

before *medio, mil, ¡qué . . . !, tal*:

> *medio litro*   half a litre   *mil pesetas*   a thousand pesetas
>
> *¡qué día!*   what a day!   *tal cosa*   such a thing

Nouns – CORE

These nouns end in –*a* but they are masculine:

> *el problema*   problem   *el futbolista*   footballer
>
> *el programa*   programme   *el clima*   climate
>
> *el síntoma*   symptom   *el día*   day
>
> *el sistema*   system   *el idioma*   language
>
> *el mapa*   map   *el tema*   theme
>
> *el pijama*   pyjamas

These nouns end in –*o* but they are feminine:

> *la foto*   photograph   *la moto*   motorcycle
>
> *la mano*   hand   *la radio*   radio

Compound nouns are masculine, e.g.:

> *el abrelatas*   tin-opener   *el sacacorchos*   corkscrew
>
> *el parabrisas*   windscreen

Some words change their meaning according to their gender, e.g.:

> *el cura*   priest   *la cura*   cure
>
> *el pendiente*   earring   *la pendiente*   slope
>
> *el policía*   policeman   *la policía*   police

To form the plural of nouns add, -*s* to an unstressed vowel and -*es* to a consonant:

> *el chico*   the boy   *el dolor*   pain
>
> *los chicos*   the boys   *los dolores*   pains
>
> *la silla*   the chair   *la flor*   flower
>
> *las sillas*   the chairs   *las flores*   flowers

However:
Words ending in -*z* change the -*z* to -*ces* in the plural, e.g.:

el lápiz pencil	*la vez* time
los lápices pencils	*las veces* times

Words ending in a stressed *-ión*, *-ón* or *-és* lose their accents in the plural, e.g.:

la canción song	*el francés* Frenchman
las canciones songs	*los franceses* the French
el montón pile	
los montones piles	

Note that the following usually denote a mixture of sexes:

los abuelos   grandparents
los hermanos   brothers and sisters
los hijos   children (i.e. sons and daughters)

Adjectives – CORE

Notice how the following adjectives agree in number and gender.

(a) Adjectives ending in –o change to reflect both number and gender:

	masculine	feminine
singular	*blanco*	*blanca*
plural	*blancos*	*blancas*

(b) Adjectives ending in -e or in a consonant do not change when feminine:

	masculine	feminine
singular	*verde*	*verde*
plural	*verdes*	*verdes*

	masculine	feminine
singular	*azul*	*azul*
plural	*azules*	*azules*

(c) Adjectives of nationality do not follow the above rule:

	masculine	feminine
singular	*español*	*española*
plural	*españoles*	*españolas*

(d) Some adjectives (***bueno, malo, alguno, ninguno, primero, tercero***) drop the letter -o before a masculine singular noun; *algún* and *ningún* require an accent:

un buen/mal hombre   a good/bad man
algún/ningún dinero   some/no money
el primer/tercer ejemplo   the first/third example

(e) *grande* becomes *gran* before a masculine singular and a feminine singular noun:

un gran hombre   a great man
una gran mujer   a great woman

(f) Some adjectives change their meaning according to their position:

before noun	after noun
su antiguo amigo his former friend	*el edificio antiguo* the ancient building
el pobre chico the poor boy unfortunate	*el chico pobre* the poor boy (i.e. without any money)
la misma cosa the same thing	*el rey mismo* the king himself

(g) *cada* (each) never changes:

   cada niño   each boy   *cada niña*   each girl

(h) *-ísimo, -ísima, -ísimos, -ísimas* can be added to adjectives after the final vowel is removed to give the meaning "extremely":

   un chico guapo   a handsome boy
   un chico guapísimo   an extremely handsome boy

Demonstrative adjectives (this, that, these, those) – CORE

Look at these examples.

este chico this boy	*esta chica* this girl
estos chicos these boys	*estas chicas* these girls
ese chico that boy	*esa chica* that girl
esos chicos those boys	*esas chicas* those girls
aquel chico that boy	*aquella chica* that girl
aquellos chicos those boys	*aquellas chicas* those girls

Notice there are two ways of saying "that" and "those". People or things which are referred to by *aquel* etc. are further away than people or things referred to by *ese* etc.:

   Me gusta ese libro pero no me gusta aquel libro.
   I like that book but I don't like that book (i.e. over there).

Possessive adjectives (my, your etc.) – CORE

Look at these examples:

mi libro my book	*mis libros* my books
tu libro your book (familiar singular)	*tus libros* your books (familiar singular)
su libro his/her book	*sus libros* his/her books
su libro your book (polite singular)	*sus libros* your books (polite singular)
nuestro hermano our brother	*nuestra hermana* our sister
nuestros hermanos our brothers	*nuestras hermanas* our sisters
vuestro hermano your book (familiar plural)	*vuestra hermana* your sister (familiar plural)

vuestros hermanos	your brothers (familiar plural)	*vuestras hermanas*	your sisters (familiar plural)
su libro	their book	*sus libros*	their books
su libro	your book (polite plural)	*sus libros*	your books (polite plural)

Adverbs – CORE AND EXTENSION

In English most adverbs end in "-ly": slowly, quickly, carefully, briefly.

To form an adverb in Spanish, take the feminine form of the adjective and add -*mente*:

lento	slow	*lentamente*	slowly
cuidadoso	careful	*cuidadosamente*	carefully
rápido	fast	*rápidamente*	quickly

Notice how to make an adverb from an adjective that ends in -*e* or a consonant:

| *breve* | brief | *brevemente* | briefly |
| *normal* | normal | *normalmente* | normally |

Some adverbs do not end in -*mente*:

bien	well	*mal*	badly
despacio	slowly	*a menudo*	often
arriba	upstairs	*abajo*	downstairs
bastante	enough; quite	*casi*	almost
de repente	suddenly	*por desgracia*	unfortunately
en seguida	immediately	*hasta*	until; even
luego	then	*pronto*	soon
siempre	always	*ya*	now; already
por tanto/por consiguiente	so (therefore)		

Comparatives and Superlatives of Adjectives and Adverbs – EXTENSION

Normally *más ... que* and *menos ... que* are used to form the comparative:

> *Él es **más** rico **que** ella.*   He is richer than she is.
> *Él es **menos** inteligente **que** ella.*   He is less intelligent than she is.

Notice these irregular forms:

| *mejor* | better | *peor* | worse |
| *mayor* | bigger/older | *menor* | smaller/younger |

más grande (bigger) and *más pequeño* (smaller) can also be used.

Notice also:

> *la calle mayor*   the main street
> *la plaza mayor*   the main square

más is used to form the superlative:

> *el libro **más** interesante que tengo*   the most interesting book that I have
> *la chica **más** guapa*   the prettiest girl

Notice the following:

> *el/la mejor, los/las mejores*   the best
> *el/la peor, los/las peores*   the worst
> *el/la mayor, los/las mayores*   the biggest/the oldest
> *el/la menor, los/las menores*   the smallest/the youngest

When using a superlative, "in" is translated by *de*:

> *el mejor jugador del equipo*   the best player in the team
> *las peores casas de la ciudad*   the worst houses in the city

Adverbs also form the comparative with *más*:

> *Tú hablas más claramente que él.*   You speak more clearly than he does.

Negatives – CORE

Learn these negatives.

> *nadie*   nobody
> *nada*   nothing
> *nunca/jamás*   never
> *ninguno,-a*   no
> *ni … ni …*   neither … nor …
> *tampoco*   (n)either

Examples:

> *No hay nadie en la calle.*   There is nobody in the street.
> *No hay nada en la calle.*   There is nothing in the street.
> *No voy nunca/no voy jamás.*   I never go.
> *No hay ningún trabajo allí.*   There is no work there.
> *Ni mi amigo ni yo lo vimos.*   Neither my friend nor I saw it.
> *No fui y ella no fue tampoco.*   I did not go and she did not go either.

When the negative word comes after the verb, *no* must be placed before the verb:

> *Nunca voy a la iglesia.*   I never go to church.
> ***No** voy nunca al colegio.*   I never go to school.

Pronouns – CORE

Direct object pronouns

Study these sentences:

> *él **me** ve*   he sees me
> *él **te** ve*   he sees you
> *él **le/lo** ve*   he sees him/it/you
> *él **la** ve*   he sees her/it/you

> *él **nos** ve*   he sees us
> *él **os** ve*   he sees you
> *él **les/los** ve*   he sees them/you
> *él **las** ve*   he sees them/you

Pronouns normally come before the verb. When there are two parts to the verb, they normally come before the first part:

Me ha visto. He has seen me.

Pronouns are attached to the end of the verb:

(a) when it is an infinitive (i.e. it ends in *-ar*, *-er* or *-ir*):

Voy a hacerlo. I am going to do it.

(b) when it is a present participle (i.e. it ends in *-ando* or *-iendo*):

Estoy haciéndolo. I am doing it (notice the accent).

(c) when it is a positive command:

¡Escúchame! Listen to me!

but **not** with negative commands:

¡no le escuches! do not listen to him!

con + *mí* becomes *conmigo* = with me
con + *ti* becomes *contigo* = with you

Personal *a* – CORE

Rule:

When the direct object of a sentence is a person, *a* is placed before the person:

Visité a Juan. I visited Juan.
Visité la catedral. I visited the cathedral.

The personal *a* is sometimes also used with regard to a pet when the speaker wishes to show affection for the animal:

¿Has visto al perro? Have you seen the dog?

Verbs – CORE

ser and *estar*

Both these verbs mean "to be". To work out which to use, the following formula is useful:

(a) In a "who" situation, use *ser*:

¿Quién es? Es nuestro profesor. Who is he? He is our teacher.
Él es francés y ella es belga. He is French and she is Belgian.

(b) In a "what" situation, use *ser*:

¿Qué es eso? Es una mesa. What's that? It's a table.

(c) In a "when" situation, use *ser*:

¿Qué hora es? Son las dos. What time is it? It is two o'clock.
¿Qué fecha es? Es el dos de mayo. What's the date? It's the second of May.
Es verano. It's summer.

(d) In a "where" situation, use *estar*:

¿Dónde está la estación? Está allí. Where is the station? It's there.

(e) In a "what like" situation, you must work out whether the description refers to a temporary characterisic or a permanent characteristic. If the characteristic is temporary use *estar*; if permanent use *ser*:

> *El cielo está azul.*   The sky is blue (i.e., but it may well change colour soon).
>
> *La puerta es azul.*   The door is blue (i.e., although it may be repainted, the colour is

a fairly permanent feature of the door).

conocer and *saber*

Both of these verbs mean "to know". *Conocer* is to know a person or a place, and *saber* is to know a fact or how to do something – in this case, it is often translated by "can":

> *Conozco Madrid muy bien.*   I know Madrid very well.
>
> *¿No conoces a María?*   Don't you know María?
>
> *Sé la hora pero no sé la fecha.*   I know the time but not the date.
>
> *Ella sabe nadar y él sabe cocinar.*   She can swim and he can cook.

Expressions with *tener*

Note these expressions which use *tener*:

tengo quince años I am fifteen	*tengo prisa* I am in a hurry
tengo calor I am hot	*tengo que ir* I have to go
tengo éxito I am successful	*tengo razón* I am right
tengo frío I am cold	*tengo sed* I am thirsty
tengo hambre I am hungry	*tengo suerte* I am lucky
tengo miedo I am frightened	

The Present Tense – CORE

The infinitives of all verbs end in either *-ar*, *-er* or *-ir*.

-ar verbs

e.g. *mirar* (to look):

> *miro*   I look
>
> *miras*   you look
>
> *mira*   he/she looks, you look
>
> *miramos*   we look
>
> *miráis*   you look
>
> *miran*   they look, you look

-er verbs

e.g. *comer* (to eat):

> *como*   I eat
>
> *comes*   you eat
>
> *come*   he/she eats, you eat
>
> *comemos*   we eat
>
> *coméis*   you eat
>
> *comen*   they eat, you eat

-ir verbs

e.g. *vivir* (to live):

> *vivo*   I live
> *vives*   you live
> *vive*   he/she lives, you live
> *vivimos*   we live
> *vivís*   you live
> *viven*   they live, you live

Radical-changing verbs

Radical-changing means that the stem of the verb changes in the first person singular, second person singular, third person singular and third person plural. There are three groups:

Group 1

Verbs that change *-e* to *-ie*; these can be *-ar* verbs, *-er* verbs or *-ir* verbs.

Group 1 *-ar* verbs

e.g *cerrar* (to close):

> *cierro*   I close
> *cierras*   you close
> *cierra*   he/she closes, you close
> *cerramos*   we close
> *cerráis*   you close
> *cierran*   they close, you close

Other Group 1 *-ar* verbs include: *despertar* (to awaken), *empezar* (to begin), *pensar* (to think), *sentarse* (to sit down), *nevar* (to snow).

Group 1 *-er* verbs

e.g. *perder* (to lose):

> *pierdo*   I lose
> *pierdes*   you lose
> *pierde*   he/she loses, you lose
> *perdemos*   we lose
> *perdéis*   you lose
> *pierden*   they lose, you lose

Other Group 1 *-er* verbs include: *encender* (to light), *entender* (to understand), *querer* (to want, to like, to love).

Group 1 *-ir* verbs

e.g. *preferir* (to prefer):

> *prefiero*   I prefer
> *prefieres*   you prefer
> *prefiere*   he/she prefers, you prefer

>   *preferimos*   we prefer
>   *preferís*   you prefer
>   *prefieren*   they prefer; you prefer

Other Group 1 *-ir* verbs include: *divertirse* (to amuse oneself), *herir* (to injure), *hervir* (to boil), *sentir* (to feel).

Group 2

Verbs that change *-o* or *-u* to *-ue*; these can be *-ar*, *-er* or *-ir* verbs.

Group 2 *-ar* verbs
e.g. *encontrar* (to meet):

>   *encuentro*   I meet
>   *encuentras*   you meet
>   *encuentra*   he/she meets, you meet
>   *encontramos*   we meet
>   *encontráis*   you meet
>   *encuentran*   they meet, you meet

Other Group 2 -ar verbs include: *acordarse* (to remember), *contar* (to tell), *costar* (to cost), *jugar* (to play), *volar* (to fly).

Group 2 *-er* verbs
e.g. *volver* (to return):

>   *vuelvo*   I return
>   *vuelves*   you return
>   *vuelve*   he/she returns, you return
>   *volvemos*   we return
>   *volvéis*   you return
>   *vuelven*   they return, you return

Other Group 2 -er verbs include: *doler* (to hurt), *poder* (to be able), *llover* (to rain).

Group 2 *-ir* verbs
e.g. *dormir* (to sleep), *morir* (to die):

>   *duermo*   I sleep
>   *duermes*   you sleep
>   *duerme*   he/she sleeps, you sleep
>   *dormimos*   we sleep
>   *dormís*   you sleep
>   *duermen*   they sleep, you sleep

Group 3

Verbs that change *-e* to *-i*; these are *-ir* verbs only.
e.g. *pedir* (to ask, ask for)

pido   I ask
pides   you ask
pide   he/she asks, you ask
pedimos   we ask
pedís   you ask
piden   they ask, you ask

Other Group 3 verbs include: *despedirse de* (to say goodbye to), *reír* (to laugh), *repetir* (to repeat), *seguir* (to follow), *vestirse* (to get dressed).

Verbs that are irregular in the present tense

Many verbs that are irregular in the present tense are only irregular in the first person singular. After that they are regular.
e.g. *hacer* (to do, make):

hago   I do, make
haces   you do, make
hace   he/she does, makes, you do,make
hacemos   we make
hacéis   you make
hacen   they make, you make

Other verbs that are irregular in the first person only are:

caer (to fall) – *caigo*, *caes* etc.
conducir (to drive) – *conduzco*, *conduces* etc.
conocer (to know) – *conozco*, *conoces* etc.
dar (to give) – *doy*, *das* etc.
ofrecer (to offer) – *ofrezco*, *ofreces* etc.
poner (to put) – *pongo*, *pones* etc.
saber (to know) – *sé*, *sabes* etc.
salir (to go out) – *salgo*, *sales* etc.
traer (to bring) – *traigo*, *traes* etc.
ver (to see) – *veo*, *ves* etc.

Other irregular verbs

decir (to say)	**huir** (to flee)	**ser** (to be)
digo	*huyo*	*soy*
dices	*huyes*	*eres*
dice	*huye*	*es*
decimos	*huimos*	*somos*
decís	*huís*	*sois*
dicen	*huyen*	*son*

estar (to be)	*ir* (to go)	*tener* (to have)
estoy	voy	tengo
estás	vas	tienes
está	va	tiene
estamos	vamos	tenemos
estáis	vais	tenéis
están	van	tienen

haber (to have)	*oír* (to hear)	*venir* (to come)
he	oigo	vengo
has	oyes	vienes
ha	oye	viene
hemos	oímos	venimos
habéis	oís	venís
han	oyen	vienen

The Perfect Tense – CORE

The perfect tense in English always has "has" or "have" in it, e.g. I have gone, they have run, he has seen.

The perfect tense in Spanish is formed by taking the present tense of *haber* and adding the participle so you need to know about *haber* and you need to know about past participles.

Present tense of *haber*

he	I have
has	you have
ha	he/she has, you have
hemos	we have
habéis	you have
han	they have, you have

Past participles

To find a past participle of a verb in English, just imagine that the words "I have" are in front of it. For example, if you want to find the past participle of the verb "to write", put "I have" in front of it. You would say "I have written", so "written" is the past participle of "to write". In the same way, "gone" is the past participle of "to go" and so on.

In Spanish, to form the past participle of an *-ar* verb, take off the *-ar* and add *-ado*. So the past participle of *hablar* is *hablado*.

To form the past participle of an *-er* or *-ir* verb, take off the *-er* or *-ir* and add *-ido*. So the past participle of *comer* is *comido* and the past participle of *vivir* is *vivido*.

Here is the perfect tense of three regular verbs:

hablar (to speak)	*comer* (to eat)	*vivir* (to live)
he hablado	he comido	he vivido
has hablado	has comido	has vivido
ha hablado	ha comido	ha vivido
hemos hablado	hemos comido	hemos vivido
habéis hablado	habéis comido	habéis vivido
han hablado	han comido	han vivido

Irregular past participles

Some past participles do not obey the rules and must be learned separately:

abrir (to open) – **abierto**		*morir* (to die) – **muerto**
cubrir (to cover) – **cubierto**		*poner* (to put) – **puesto**
decir (to say) – **dicho**		*romper* (to break) – **roto**
descubrir (to discover) – **descubierto**		*ver* (to see) – **visto**
escribir (to write) – **escrito**		*volver* (to return) – **vuelto**
hacer (to do/make) – **hecho**		

The Preterite – CORE

The preterite is sometimes known as the simple past. It is used to tell about events in the past, e.g. I went, you ran, they bought.

Here is the preterite of three regular verbs. Note that there are two sets of endings, one for *-ar* verbs and one for *-er* and *-ir* verbs.

hablar	*comer*	*vivir*
hablé	comí	viví
hablaste	comiste	viviste
habló	comió	vivió
hablamos	comimos	vivimos
hablasteis	comisteis	vivisteis
hablaron	comieron	vivieron

Note that the role played in English by "did" in the negative and question forms of the preterite is not reflected in Spanish:

hablé	I spoke
no hablé	I did not speak
¿hablé?	did I speak?

Radical-changing verbs in the preterite

There are **no** *-ar* or *-er* radical-changing verbs in the preterite.

Some *-ir* verbs change *-e* to *-i* in the third persons singular and plural. Some of these verbs are: *pedir* (to ask for), *preferir* (to prefer), *reír* (to laugh), *seguir* (to follow), *sentir* (to feel), *sonreír* (to smile), *vestirse* (to get dressed).

For example, *pedir*:

> *pedí*
> *pediste*
> *pidió*
> *pedimos*
> *pedisteis*
> *pidieron*

Note what happens to the first person singular of verbs that end in **-zar**, **-gar** and **-car**:

empezar (to start)	*empecé*
jugar (to play)	*jugué*
buscar (to look for)	*busqué*

You should learn the preterite of *caer* (to fall):

> *caí*
> *caíste*
> *cayó*
> *caímos*
> *caísteis*
> *cayeron*

Irregular preterites

dar (to give):

> *di*
> *diste*
> *dio*
> *dimos*
> *disteis*
> *dieron*

ser (to be) and **ir** (to go) have the same preterite:

> *fui*
> *fuiste*
> *fue*
> *fuimos*
> *fuisteis*
> *fueron*

Pretéritos graves

These are irregular and are called *grave* because the stress in the first and third persons singular does not fall as it usually does on the last syllable, but on the second to last.

andar (to walk)	***decir*** (to say)	***estar*** (to be)
anduve	dije	estuve
anduviste	dijiste	estuviste
anduvo	dijo	estuvo
anduvimos	dijimos	estuvimos
anduvisteis	dijisteis	estuvisteis
anduvieron	dijeron	estuvieron

haber (to have)	***hacer*** (to do/make)	***poder*** (to be able)
hube	hice	pude
hubiste	hiciste	pudiste
hubo	hizo	pudo
hubimos	hicimos	pudimos
hubisteis	hicisteis	pudisteis
hubieron	hicieron	pudieron

poner (to put)	***querer*** (to want)	***saber*** (to know)
puse	quise	supe
pusiste	quisiste	supiste
puso	quiso	supo
pusimos	quisimos	supimos
pusisteis	quisisteis	supisteis
pusieron	quisieron	supieron

tener (to have)	***traer*** (to bring)	***venir*** (to come)
tuve	traje	vine
tuviste	trajiste	viniste
tuvo	trajo	vino
tuvimos	trajimos	vinimos
tuvisteis	trajisteis	vinisteis
tuvieron	trajeron	vinieron

The Imperfect Tense – CORE

The imperfect tense is used for things that used to happen or were happening, e.g. I used to play football, I was going to the cinema. It is often used to describe situations in the past, e.g. it was raining, she was wearing a coat.

To form the imperfect, add one of two sets of endings to the stem of the verb as follows (the *-aba* endings are for *-ar* verbs and the *-ía* endings are for *-er* and *-ir* verbs):

hablar	comer	vivir
hablaba	comía	vivía
hablabas	comías	vivías
hablaba	comía	vivía
hablábamos	comíamos	vivíamos
hablabais	comíais	vivíais
hablaban	comían	vivían

Irregular imperfects

There are only three irregular imperfects:

ir (to go)	*ser* (to be)	*ver* (to see)
iba	era	veía
ibas	eras	veías
iba	era	veía
íbamos	éramos	veíamos
ibais	erais	veíais
iban	eran	veían

The Future Tense – CORE

The future tense is used to describe future events – the meaning conveyed in English by the words "will" and "shall", e.g. I shall see, they will go.

To form the future tense in Spanish, you add endings to the infinitive. There is only one set of endings for the future: *-é, -ás, -á, -emos, -éis, -án.*

Regular futures

hablar	comer	vivir
hablaré	comeré	viviré
hablarás	comerás	vivirás
hablará	comerá	vivirá
hablaremos	comeremos	viviremos
hablaréis	comeréis	viviréis
hablarán	comerán	vivirán

Irregular futures

Note that the endings are the same as those of the regular forms.

decir (to say)	*haber* (to have)	*hacer* (to do, to make)
diré	habré	haré
dirás	habrás	harás
dirá	habrá	hará
diremos	habremos	haremos
diréis	habréis	haréis
dirán	habrán	harán

poder (to be able)	*poner* (to put)	*querer* (to want)
podré	pondré	querré
podrás	pondrás	querrás
podrá	pondrá	querrá
podremos	pondremos	querremos
podréis	pondréis	querréis
podrán	pondrán	querrán

saber (to know)	*salir* (to go out)	*tener* (to have)
sabré	saldré	tendré
sabrás	saldrás	tendrás
sabrá	saldrá	tendrá
sabremos	saldremos	tendremos
sabréis	saldréis	tendréis
sabrán	saldrán	tendrán

venir (to come)
vendré
vendrás
vendrá
vendremos
vendréis
vendrán

The Conditional – EXTENSION

This is recognised in English by the use of the word "would" or, sometimes, "should", e.g. I would go, I should like etc.

In Spanish you form the conditional by adding the endings used for the imperfect of *-er* and *-ir* verbs to the infinitive, e.g. *hablaría* I would speak, *iría* I would go.

hablar	*comer*	*vivir*
hablaría	comería	viviría
hablarías	comerías	vivirías
hablaría	comería	viviría
hablaríamos	comeríamos	viviríamos
hablaríais	comeríais	viviríais
hablarían	comerían	vivirían

Irregular conditionals

The same verbs that are irregular in the future are irregular in the conditional. The irregular conditionals use the same stems as the irregular futures.

decir (to say)	*haber* (to have)	*hacer* (to do, to make)
diría	habría	haría
dirías	habrías	harías
diría	habría	haría
diríamos	habríamos	haríamos
diríais	habríais	haríais
dirían	habrían	harían

poder (to be able)	*poner* (to put)	*querer* (to want)
podría	pondría	querría
podrías	pondrías	querrías
podría	pondría	querría
podríamos	pondríamos	querríamos
podríais	pondríais	querríais
podrían	pondrían	querrían

saber (to know)	*salir* (to go out)	*tener* (to have)
sabría	saldría	tendría
sabrías	saldrías	tendrías
sabría	saldría	tendría
sabríamos	saldríamos	tendríamos
sabríais	saldríais	tendríais
sabrían	saldrían	tendrían

venir (to come)
vendría
vendrías
vendría
vendríamos
vendríais
vendrían

Pluperfect tense – EXTENSION

This is recognised in English by the word "had". The pluperfect is used for things that had happened, e.g he had seen, they had gone. To form the pluperfect in Spanish, take the imperfect of *haber* and add the past participle, e.g. *había hablado* I had spoken, *habíamos ido al teatro* we had been to the theatre.

hablar	*comer*	*vivir*
había hablado	había comido	había vivido
habías hablado	habías comido	habías vivido
había hablado	había comido	había vivido
habíamos hablad	habíamos comido	habíamos vivido
habíais hablado	habíais comido	habíais vivido
habían hablado	habían comido	habían vivido

7 – Practice Examination Paper

LISTENING

When you hear the pause signal, pause the tape.
When you hear the repeat signal, rewind to the beginning of the exercise.

Section 1: Foundation

Exercise 1:   Questions 1–5

In this exercise you will hear some short remarks in Spanish. Answer each question by ticking one box only.

Example:

You arrive at Madrid airport and ask the best way to get to the city centre.

¿El centro? Toma un autobús.

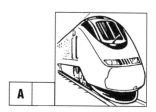 A

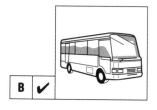 B ✔

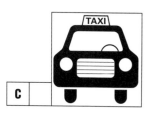 C

---

1   You ask someone the way to the Hotel Sol. Which way should you go?

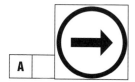 A

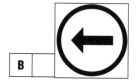 B

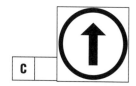 C

[1]

2   In the hotel you ask the price of a room. What is the reply?

A 5 500 ☐   **B** 4 400 ☐   **C** 6 200 ☐

[1]

3 What facility in your room are you told about?

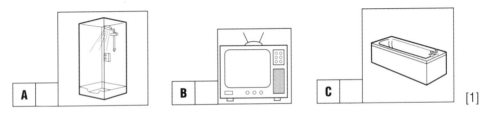

A   B   C   [1]

4 You want to know what time the restaurant opens. What is the reply?

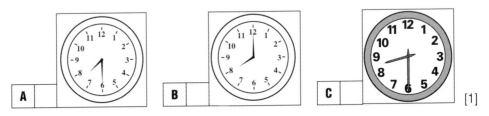

A   B   C   [1]

5 What problem are you told about?

A   B   C   [1]

[Total: 5 marks]

Ejercicio 2:   Preguntas 6–15

Ana habla de su familia.

Marca una señal (✔) en la casilla correcta.

Ejemplo: ¿Cuántos años tiene Ana?

A 15 ☐   **B** 16 ✔   **C** 17 ☐

La respuesta correcta es **B**.

6 Ana tiene

A   B   C

7 También tiene

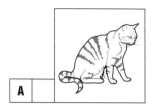
A

B

C

8 El trabajo de su padre

A

B

C

9 El trabajo de su madre

A

B

C

10 El pasatiempo de Ana

A

B

C

11 Su asignatura favorita

A

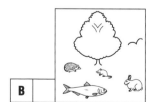
B

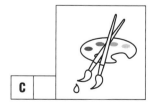
C

12 Ana vuelve a casa

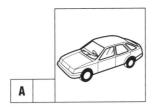 A

 B

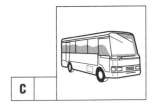 C

13 Su casa está

 A

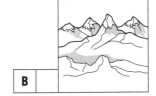 B

 C

14 Ana ayuda en casa.

 A

 B

 C

15 Por la tarde Ana ...

 A

 B

 C

[Total: 10 marks]

Ejercicio 3: Preguntas 16–20

¿Dónde está Paco? Marca una señal (✔) en la casilla correcta.

Ejemplo:

 A ✔

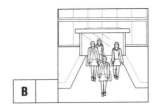 B

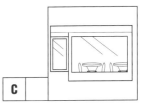 C

La respuesta correcta es **A**.

16   Paco va

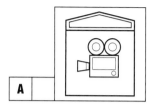 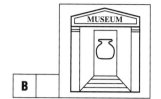 

17   Paco pasa sus vacaciones

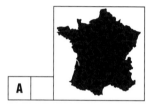  

18   Paco duerme en

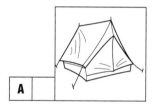  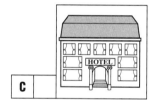

19   Paco está

 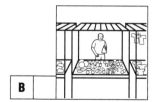 

20   Paco visita

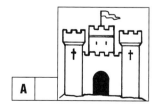 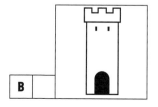 

[Total: 5 marks]

Ejercicio 4: Preguntas 21–25

Seis jóvenes hablan de cómo ayudan en casa.

 Escribe la letra correcta en la casilla.

Ejemplo:

Marco ...*A*.......

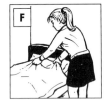

21 Ana ☐ [1] **24** José ☐ [1]

22 Luis ☐ [1] **25** David ☐ [1]

23 Cristina ☐ [1]

[Total 5 marks]

Ejercicio 5: Preguntas 26–30

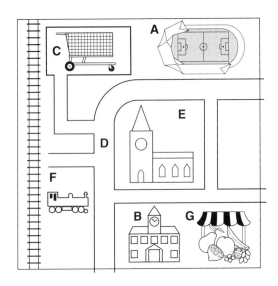

Isabel describe el pueblo. ¿De qué habla?

Escribe la letra que corresponde.

Ejemplo:

La respuesta correcta es [A]

📖 Mira el plano.

Escucha.

26	☐	[1]
27	☐	[1]
28	☐	[1]
29	☐	[1]
30	☐	[1]

[Total: 5 marks]

[Total for Section: 30]

Section 2: Common Exercises

Exercise 1:   Questions 1–5

Lolita is talking about what she did last night.

📖 Answer the questions **in English**.

Example: Where does Lolita work?

.... *supermarket* ....

1 What was wrong with Lolita when she got home?

.... [1]

2 What was it that made Lolita feel better?

.... [1]

3 How was Lolita feeling now?

.... [1]

4 What is El Tulipán?

.... [1]

5 Why did Lolita feel happy when she arrived?

.... [1]

[Total: 5 marks]

Ejercicio 2: Preguntas 6–12

Escucha a estos españoles hablando de su futuro. Mira la lista de descripciones. No necesitarás todas las letras. 📼

Ejemplo:

Rocío

La respuesta correcta es **D**.

Los jóvenes

6 Alvaro ☐

7 María ☐

8 Clara ☐

9 Susi ☐

10 Carlos ☐

11 Pedro ☐

12 Jaime ☐

Ambiciones

A Quiere ser periodista

B Quiere trabajar con ordenadores

C Quiere cocinar

D Quiere ser deportista

E Quiere ser profesor/profesora

F Quiere trabajar en el campo

G Quiere ser arquitecto/arquitecta

H Quiere ser autor

I Quiere trabajar en el extranjero

[Total: 7 marks]

Ejercicio 3: Preguntas 13–16

En la radio: el pronóstico del tiempo 📼

 Escribe la letra que corresponde. No necesitarás todas las letras.

Ejemplo:

Madrid A B

Las respuestas correctas son **A** y **B**.

Escucha.

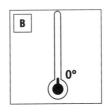

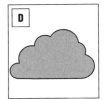

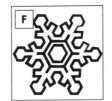

13 Barcelona ☐ y ☐   [2]

14 Cádiz ☐ y ☐   [2]

15 Santiago ☐ y ☐   [2]

16 Málaga ☐ y ☐   [2]

[Total: 8 marks]

[Total for Section: 20]

Section 3: Higher

Ejercicio 1: Preguntas 1–10

En la radio. ¿De qué se habla?

Escribe la letra que corresponde mejor. No necesitarás todas las letras.

Ejemplo:

La respuesta correcta es **B**.

A Política	**B** Un accidente	**C** Desastre natural
D Un robo	**E** Un cumpleaños	**F** Lotería
G Huelga	**H** Una separación	**I** Un nacimiento
J Deporte	**K** Empleos nuevos	**J** Una enfermedad

1 ☐   2 ☐

3 ☐   4 ☐

5 ☐   6 ☐

7 ☐   8 ☐

9 ☐   10 ☐

[Total: 10 marks]

Ejercicio 2: Preguntas 11–20

Un español describe su vida en Nueva York. Marca un señal (✔) en la casilla correcta.

Ejemplo: ¿En qué parte de Nueva York vive Francisco?

A vive lejos del centro ☐

B vive en un barrio céntrico ✔

C vive cerca del centro ☐

Escucha.

11 Una ventaja de la vida en Nueva York

A el clima ☐

B hay muchos españoles ☐

C hablar inglés no es tan importante ☐ [1]

12 ¿Cuándo emigró Francisco?

A recientemente ☐

B cuando era joven ☐

C cuando tenía veinte años ☐ [1]

13 ¿Quién le acompañó a Nueva York?

A nadie ☐

B su familia ☐

C su mujer ☐ [1]

14 ¿En qué trabaja Francisco?

A es jardinero ☐

B es ingeniero ☐

C es obrero ☐ [1]

15 ¿Cuál es su estado civil ahora?

A es soltero ☐

B tiene una esposa ☐

C va a casarse ☐ [1]

16 ¿Cuál era su primer trabajo en Nueva York?

A era jardinero ☐

B era ingeniero ☐

C era obrero ☐ [1]

17 ¿Qué pasó con su primer patrón?

    A emigró   ☐

    B perdió su trabajo   ☐

    C le asesinaron   ☐   [1]

18 ¿Va a volver a España?

    A quizás   ☐

    B nunca   ☐

    C seguramente   ☐   [1]

19 Y ¿la violencia en Nueva York?

    A hay más que en España   ☐

    B hay menos que en España   ☐

    C es igual que en España   ☐   [1]

20 ¿Por qué Francisco no teme la violencia?

    A porque tiene una pistola   ☐

    B porque sólo sale de día   ☐

    C porque tiene muchos amigos   ☐   [1]

[Total: 10 marks]

Ejercicio 3:   Preguntas 21–25

Felipe habla de su empleo de vacaciones.

Contesta **en español**.

    Ejemplo:
    ¿Cuánto tiempo trabajaba Felipe?

    ..... *Un mes* .....

Escucha.

21 ¿En dónde trabajaba Felipe?

    .... [1]

22 ¿Por qué no estaba contento Felipe la segunda semana?

    .... [1]

23 ¿Por qué el hotel no estaba completo la segunda semana?

.... [1]

24 ¿Qué dijo Reyes?

.... [1]

25 ¿Por qué dejó Felipe el trabajo?

.... [1]

[Total: 5 marks]

Exercise 4:   Questions 26–30

A young man is having problems with his girlfriend.

Answer **in English**.

Example: For how long has he gone out with Carmen?

...... *2 years* ....

Listen to what the young man says.

26 Give **three** reasons why Carmen is furious with her young man.

.... [1]

.... [1]

.... [1]

27 Which of the three complaints does the young man feel is unjustified?

.... [1]

28 How does the young man know that his efforts at making peace have failed?

.... [1]

[Total: 5 marks]

[Total for Section: 30]

READING

Section 1: Foundation

Exercise 1   Questions 1–5

Answer each question by ticking one box only.

Example: You want to go to the station. Which sign do you follow?

A ☐ Ayuntamiento ⇨

B ☐ Hotel ⇨

C ☑ Estación ⇨

Answer: *C, Estación*

Now answer these questions.

You are in Spain. Which sign do you look for?

1 You want to buy some petrol

A ☐ Gasolina ⇨

B ☐ Mercado ⇨

C ☐ Estación ⇨   [1]

2 You want to post a letter

A ☐ Zapatería ⇨

B ☐ Correos ⇨

C ☐ Panadería ⇨   [1]

3 You want to go to the town centre

A ☐ Ayuntamiento ⇨

B ☐ Hotel ⇨

C ☐ Centro de la ciudad ⇨   [1]

4 You want to buy some bread

A ☐ Panadería ⇨

B ☐ Periódicos ⇨

C ☐ Estación ⇨   [1]

5 You want to buy a magazine

A ☐ Tarjetas postales ⇨

B ☐ Revistas ⇨

C ☐ Banco ⇨   [1]

[Total: 5 marks]

Ejercicio 2:   Preguntas 6–10

Hay tres campings. ¿Qué instalaciones hay? Escribe letra A, B o C en la casilla.

A

Camping Oviedo

– agua caliente
– piscina
– bar
– restaurante
– cerrado en invierno

B

Camping Sevilla

– agua caliente
– canchas de tenis y terrenos de fútbol
– playa a 100 metros
– bar
– cerrado en invierno
– sitio para 200 tiendas

C

Camping Lérida

– agua caliente
– bar
– abierto todo el año
– sitios para caravanas y tiendas

Ejemplo: Tienes una caravana   ☐ *C*

6 Quieres ir en diciembre   ☐   [1]

7 Quieres estar cerca del mar   ☐   [1]

8 Quieres hacer deportes   ☐   [1]

9 Quieres nadar pero no en el mar ☐ [1]

10 Quieres comer en el restaurante ☐ [1]

[Total: 5 marks]

Ejercicio 3:   Preguntas 11–15

En un restaurante, lees el menú.

Restaurante El Tulipán
Menú

Platos		**Bebidas**	
Pescado	1050	Cerveza	350
Pollo	1500	Vino	600
Sopa de tomate	700	CocaCola	850
Bistec	2000		
Patatas fritas	475	**Postre**	
		Queso	950
Fruta		Helado	1250
Naranja	250		
Piña	300		
Plátano	400		

¿Cuánto cuesta? Escribe el precio.

Ejemplo

950
....

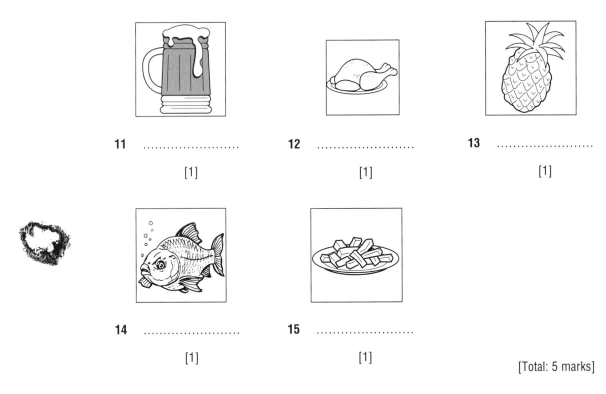

11 ....

[1]

12 ....

[1]

13 ....

[1]

14 ....

[1]

15 ....

[1]

[Total: 5 marks]

Ejercicio 4:   Preguntas 16–20

Entras en unos grandes almacenes y ves un letrero.

```
7  Todo para el ordenador
6  Ropa de mujeres
5  Ropa de hombres
4  Todo para la cocina
3  Artículos eléctricos
2  Muebles
1  Objetos perdidos
```

Escribe el número del piso que buscas.

Ejemplo: Quieres compar una falda   6

16 Quieres comprar una radio   [1]

17 Quieres comprar un sofá   [1]

18 Quieres comprar un videojuego   [1]

19 Quieres comprar sartenes y cacerolas   [1]

20 Pierdes algo en los almacenes   [1]

[Total: 5 marks]

Ejercicio 5:   Preguntas 21–30

Lee esta carta.

> *Rosa, mi amor:*
>
> *Las vacaciones no van bien. Tengo dos semanas de vacaciones: hoy es miércoles, el tercer día y ya me aburro. Está lloviendo a chorros, mi perro está enfermo, mis amigos están fuera y aquí estoy, viendo la tele.*
>
> *Me gustaría estar en los Estados Unidos contigo. Supongo que estás tomando el sol como siempre. Me quedé aquí para estudiar pero no he hecho nada.*
>
> *Bueno, hasta pronto, mi queridísima. De repente tengo hambre. Al menos la nevera está llena.*
>
> *Luis*

Ejemplo: ¿Quién es Rosa?

A la madre de Luis ☐   **B** la hermana de Luis ☐   C la novia de Luis ✔

21
Duración de sus vacaciones

A 14 días ☐   **B** 28 días ☐   **C** 7 días ☐   [1]

22
El primer día de sus vacaciones

A lunes ☐   **B** martes ☐   **C** miércoles ☐   [1]

23 El tiempo

 A   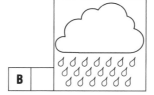 B   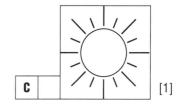 C   [1]

24 ¿Quién no se ve bien?

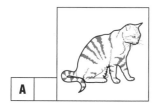 A    B   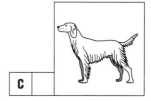 C   [1]

25 ¿Qué hace Luis?

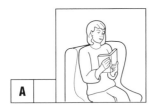   [1]

26 Destino preferido de Luis

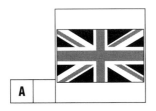 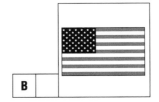 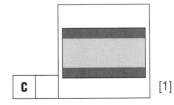 [1]

27 Ocupación preferida de Rosa

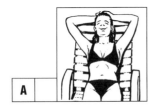   [1]

28 Lo que debe hacer Luis

   [1]

29 Tiempo pasado hasta ahora haciendo lo que debe hacer

A 2 horas ☐   **B** 0 horas ☐   **C** 6 horas ☐   [1]

30 ¿Qué va a hacer Luis ahora?

   [1]

[Total: 10 marks]
[Total for Section: 30]

Section 2: Common Exercises

Exercise 1:   Questions 1–5

You receive this e-mail from your Mexican friend.

Hola Ana

Tengo buenas noticias. ¿Te acuerdas de José? Pues anoche me llamó y dijo que quería salir conmigo. Fuimos a ver una película. Se trata de un monstruo que mata a chicas guapas en un cementerio. Durante la sesión José quiso darme un beso. Dije que no ¡claro! Después fuimos a comer calamares en un bar. Me invitó a una fiesta pasado mañana. Pues nada más. Mándame tus noticias. Tengo que ir a planchar la ropa de toda la familia. ¡Qué rollo!

Clara

Answer the questions by ticking the correct box.

Example:

José called

A last night   ☑

B today   ☐

C the day before yesterday   ☐

1 The film they saw was

   A a romantic film   ☐

   B a horror film   ☐

   C a western   ☐   [1]

2 During the film

   A José did not want a kiss   ☐

   B they both wanted to kiss   ☐

   C Clara did not want a kiss   ☐   [1]

3 After the film they ate

   A seafood   ☐

   B vegetarian food   ☐

   C fish and chips   ☐   [1]

4 The party is

   A in two days' time   ☐

   B today   ☐

   C tomorrow   ☐   [1]

5 Clara has to go and do

   A homework   ☐

   B housework   ☐

   C gardening   ☐   [1]

[Total: 5 marks]

Ejercicio 2:   Preguntas 6–13

Lee este mensaje.

> Esteban,
>
> Mi tía me ha escrito. Dice que ya no puede visitarnos en Pascuas porque su marido tiene que ir a Alemania para trabajar. Prefiere venir aquí con su marido. Dice que probablemente vendrá en julio o agosto.
>
> Como mi tía no viene, ahora puedo ir contigo a la montaña. ¿Aún tienes planes para hacer alpinismo en las montañas? Me encantaría hacer esto.
>
> Conchita

Ahora rellena los espacios para dar el sentido del mensaje, escogiendo las palabras de la lista.

Esteban es el … *amigo* …… de Conchita

Conchita ha recibido una **6** ………….. de una **7** ………………

Esa persona no puede ir a verla en semana **8** …………. porque su marido se va al

9 ……………… Ahora quiere venir en **10** ………….. Conchita quiere **11** ………….. a Estaban a

la montaña para **12** ………. montañas. Espera la ocasión con mucha **13** …………..

extranjero	América	impaciencia	pariente	padre	santa	primavera
verano	acompañar	bajar	subir	amigo carta	llamada	amiga

[Total: 8 marks]

Ejercicio 3:   Preguntas 14–20

Imagina que estás en estas situaciones. ¿Qué decisiones tomarás?
Escribe la letra correcta en la casilla.

Ejemplo:
Situación: Tienes sed   Decisión: $\boxed{H}$

Situaciones

14	Quieres ir de vacaciones pero no tienes dinero	☐
15	Tienes ganas de dormir	☐
16	Quieres adelgazar	☐
17	Tu hermana se ha roto el dedo	☐
18	Estás en tu instituto y hay un incendio	☐
19	Quieres aprender portugés	☐
20	Tienes hambre y no quieres comer ni carne ni pescado	☐

Decisiones

A   Llévala al hospital
B   Buscas trabajo
C   Busca una salida
D   Te acuestas
E   Vete a una escuela de idiomas
F   Cómprate una bicicleta
G   Cómprate comida vegetariana
H   Bebe una cocacola

[Total: 7 marks]
[Total for section:20]

Section 3: Higher

Ejercicio 1:   Preguntas 1–10

Lee estos anuncios.

¿Averiado? ¿Problemas con tu coche? Llama Paco – 2 43 22 22

El martes, trece de octubre hubo un accidente en la calle Goya a las 11.00. Si Vd. vio el accidente, llame por favor. Pedro 4 16 43 38

El Señor don Rafael Alonso, ex-alcalde de esta ciudad, ha fallecido el 15 de octubre. El entierro tendrá lugar mañana martes.

Coches nuevos. Ahorre dinero comprando en Portugal. Yo busco el coche que Vd. escoge y hago todo el papeleo. Llame Gerardo 3 45 56 13

Busco terreno para viviendas y pisos. Pago en metálico en el acto Esteban 2 34 54 23

Elena. Discúlpame. Fue culpa mía. Llama a Patricio 3 43 24 98

Hermanos Cabral. La mejor autoescuela de España. Llame a Ana 9 63 346 37

¿No quieres hacer cola? ¿No quieres esperar? Ofrezco peinados en su casa a toda hora. Lolita 2 34 53 23

¿Tocas la batería? "Los lobos", grupo rock te busca. Llama Sheila – 2 34 56 11

La boda de Carlos Herráiz y Maite Jiménez se celebrará el lunes en la iglesia de San Miguel.

Compro anillos, pendientes y collares. Llame Alvaro – 2 32 56 76

Ejemplo ¿Quién repara coches?	Paco	Pedro	Rafael	Gerardo	Esteban	Patricio	Elena	Ana	Lolita	Sheila	Maite	Alvaro
	✔											
1 ¿Quién importa autos?												
2 ¿Quién busca testigos?												
3 ¿Quién compra metales de valor?												
4 ¿Quién murió?												
5 ¿Quién pide perdón?												
6 ¿Quién es músico/a?												
7 ¿Quién es peluquero/a?												
8 ¿Quién enseña a conducir?												
9 ¿Quién se casa?												
10 ¿Quién es constructor/a?												

[Total: 10 marks]

Ejercicio 2:   Preguntas 11–15

Lee este anuncio.

> ## ¡Jóvenes!
> ### Trabaja en Israel/Palestina/Arabia Saudí
> - sueldo magnífico
> - piso pagado
> - coche
> - 40 horas semanales (máximo)
> - clima excepcional
> - trabajo peligroso y duro (construcción)
> - sólo solteros

Empareja las frases.

Ejemplo:

Casi siempre hace   ....*B*........

The correct answer is   *B*

11 El anuncio ofrece trabajo en ....   A el Medio Oriente

                                                       B excepcional

12 No tienes que trabajar ....   C fácil

                                                       D personas casadas

13 No se aceptan ....   E horas suplementarias

                                                       F buen tiempo

14 El trabajo no es ....

15 La paga es ....

[Total: 5 marks]

Ejercicio 3   Preguntas 16–25

Lee esta carta y contesta **en español**.

Asturias, 6 junio

Querido Paul:

¿Cómo estás después de tu operación de apendicitis? ¡Que te mejores! Me dicen que vuelves a casa pronto.

Me encuentro aquí en Asturias. Es un viaje de fin de curso y lo pasamos muy bien.

Ahorré todo el año y tuve que hacer un trabajito. Limpié los cristales en una urbanización cercana. Lo bueno era el dinero. Pero tuve que comprar una escalera.

En Asturias, busqué gangas, claro, y compré blusas y camisas de seda para mis amigos.

Oviedo es un paraíso y comemos como reyes pero lo malo es el olor que viene del río.

Hicimos un paseo en la montaña. ¡Vimos lobos! Según una amiga, el lobo está en peligro de extinción porque su alimentación se basa en ovejas y ¡puedes imaginarte la reacción de los granjeros! Según esta amiga, el lobo se protege por su velocidad. Un lobo alcanza una velocidad de 45km/h.

Entonces, hasta pronto

Dolores

Ejemplo:

¿La fecha de la carta?

  el 6 de junio

16 ¿Dónde está Paul ahora?

.... [1]

17 Dolores está en Oviedo. ¿Qué está celebrando?

.... [1]

18 ¿Por qué compró Dolores una escalera?

.... [1]

19 ¿Qué material parece barato en Asturias?

.... [1]

20 En Oviedo, ¿qué cosa impresionó a Dolores?

.... [1]

21 En Oviedo, ¿qué cosa no impresionó a Dolores?

.... [1]

22 Dolores dio una vuelta en Oviedo. ¿Dónde exactamente?

.... [1]

23 A los granjeros no les gustan los lobos. ¿Por qué?

.... [1]

24 ¿Qué ventaja natural tienen los lobos?

.... [1]

25 ¿Cuántos kilómetros por hora puede correr un lobo?

.... [1]

[Total: 10 marks]

Exercise 4:   Questions 26 –30

Read this interview with a film star, then answer each question by ticking **one box only**.

Christian García: Su película se estrena ahora en España

Su padre, Roger García fue uno de los cineastas más famosos de los años setenta.
¿Qué opina usted ahora de todo aquello?
La generación de mi padre se lo pasó bomba. Se divirtieron como locos. Ahora la gente se instala en el sofá con el mando a distancia en la mano, y sin hablar se divierte entre cuatro paredes.

Sus padres eran salvajes y impulsivos. ¿Y usted?

Mi padre se reía de todo, del bien y del mal. Yo, normalmente reflexiono antes de actuar.

La película se rodó en medio de la montaña. ¿Le resultó especialmente duro trabajar en esas condiciones?

Lo más duro fue que no podía llamar. Allí sólo había dos líneas y todo el equipo nos peleábamos por ellas.

Y ¿su hermana Chiara?

La quiero mucho pero la veo poco. Es mi mejor abogada.

¿Quién le ha ayudado más en su familia?

Este tipo de comparaciones me resultan bastante difíciles. Por un lado, mi primer trabajo en el cine me lo dio mi padre. Mi hermana, la quiero mucho pero mi madre es la que más consejos me da.

26   According to Christian, how do people spend their leisure time?

    A   Watching TV   ☐

    B   Chatting at home   ☐

    C   They like to go out   ☐   [1]

27   What kind of person is Christian?

    A   He acts on impulse   ☐

    B   He never takes the initiative   ☐

    C   He thinks before he acts   ☐   [1]

28   What was it that the film crew could not do easily?

    A   Work   ☐

    B   Travel   ☐

    C   Phone   ☐   [1]

29   How does he feel about his sister?

    A   He loves her and knows she is supportive   ☐

    B   He loves her but knows she does not support him   ☐

    C   He does not love her   ☐   [1]

30   Who does he feel gave him most advice?

    A   His father   ☐

    B   His mother   ☐

    C   His sister   ☐   [1]

[Total: 5 marks]

[Total for Section: 30]

SPEAKING

Section 1: Foundation

You are in a restaurant with a friend.

You will need to:

- ask for a table for two
- ask for the menu of the day
- order two lemonades or any other drinks
- ask for chicken or any other meat dish

Your teacher will play the part of the waiter/waitress and will start the conversation.

Section 2: Common Exercises

You are working in a hotel. A Spaniard asks you about your job.

You will need to:

- mention how long you have worked in the hotel
- say how much you earn
- mention 2 things that you have to do
- answer a question

Your teacher will play the part of the Spaniard and will start the conversation.

Section 3: Higher

The notes and pictures on the next page give an outline of events during an exchange visit to Spain last year when you stayed with Juana. Tell the examiner what happened. You need not mention every detail but you must mention the main events. Any reasonable interpretation of the icons will be accepted.

El primer día

La llegada. ¿A qué hora? ¿Transporte del aeropuerto a la casa de la familia? ¿Qué tiempo hacía?

La familia

¿Cómo es el padre de Juana? Y Juana. ¿Cómo es? ¿Y su hermano? La cena. ¿Qué cenaste? ¿Tus impresiones?

Una excursión

¿Adónde? ¿Qué hiciste? ¿Qué regalos? ¿Para quiénes?

El fin de semana

La fiesta

Una persona especial ¿Qué hicisteis durante la fiesta? ¿Quiénes interrumpieron la fiesta?

¿Qué actividades?

WRITING

Section 1: Foundation

Answer **all** questions.

Exercise 1

You are going on holiday. Write eight items that you might take with you (e.g. clothes, acessories, reading material).

Write **in Spanish**.

Example: *radio*

1 .... [1]

2 .... [1]

3 .... [1]

4 .... [1]

5 .... [1]

6 .... [1]

7 .... [1]

8 .... [1]

[Total: 8 marks]

Exercise 2

What do you do at the weekend? Where?

Fill in the gaps in Spanish with a phrase or sentence suggested by the picture.

Example:

Yo juego al tenis   *en el parque*

1 Yo ....   **2** ....   **3** Yo ....   **4** ....

5 Yo ....   **6** Yo ....

Section 2: Common Exercises

Contesta **UNA** pregunta solamente. Escoge o la pregunta 1 o la pregunta 2.

Escribe 90–100 palabras **en español**.

1 Tu amigo español quiere una descripción de tu colegio y tu rutina diaria. Escribe un e-mail a tu amigo.

Menciona:

- lo que haces durante el día (¿a qué hora empiezas?, ¿la hora de comer?)
- lo que pasó en tu colegio hoy (¿una clase mala?, ¿deporte?)
- lo qué harás mañana en tu colegio (¿una excursión?, ¿una disputa?)
- tus opiniones de tu colegio (¿los profesores?, ¿las instalaciones?)

2 Escribe una carta a tu amiga española, Lolita, describiendo las vacaciones que acabas de pasar en Escocia.

Menciona:

- el viaje a Escocia (¿cómo?, ¿con quienes?)
- las actividades (¿el tiempo?, ¿regalos?)
- tus impresiones de Escocia (¿la gente?, ¿las costumbres?)
- tus planes para las vacaciones del año que viene (¿adónde?, ¿con Lolita?)

Section 3: Higher

Contesta **UNA** pregunta solamente. Escoge o la pregunta 1 o la pregunta 2.

Escribe 140–150 palabras **en español**.

1 Acabas de volver de un intercambio en España. Escribe un informe sobre tu visita.

Menciona todos estos puntos.

- cómo viajaste y qué tal el viaje
- las cosas que pasaron durante tu estancia
- tus impresiones de los estudiantes en el instituto español
- lo que pasará cuando los españoles vengan a Inglaterra

2 Estás en España y sufres un robo. Tienes que escribir un informe para la policía.

Menciona todos estos puntos:

- dónde estabas y qué hacías

- los detalles del robo y una descripción del ladrón

- tus impresiones de la policía española

- lo que harás para resolver el problema ocasionado por el robo

[Total: 30 marks]

Answers

Listening

Section 1, Exercise 1:   1B   2A   3A   4C   5A

Ejercicio 2:   6A   7B   8C   9B   10C   11A   12B   13C   14C   15B

Ejercicio 3:   16A   17B   18A   19C   20B

Ejercicio 4:   21E   22G   23F   24D   25B

Ejercicio 5:   26E   27C   28D   29B   30F

Section 2, Exercise 1:   1 headache   2 bath   3 hungry   4 restaurant   5 met a friend

Ejercicio 2:   6C   7E   8B   9A   10G   11I   12H

Ejercicio 3:   13EJ   14DC   15IF   16GH

Section 3, Ejercicio 1:   1A   2D   3C   4E   5F   6G   7K   8H   9I   10J

Ejercicio 2:   11C   12B   13A   14C   15B   16A   17C   18A   19C   20B

Ejercicio 3:   21 *en un hotel*   22 *se aburría*   23 *las vacaciones escolares habían terminado* 24 *dijo que quería salir con Felipe*   25 *porque Reyes se había ido*

Exercise 4:   26 He is not spending the summer with her. He never pays. He is always late. 27 He is not spending the summer with her.   28 The flowers are in the bin.

Reading

Section 1, Exercise 1:   1A   2B   3C   4A   5b

Ejercicio 2:   6C   7B   8B   9A   10A

Ejercicio 3:   11 350   12 1500   13 300   14 1050   15 475

Ejercicio 4:   16 3   17 2   18 7   19 4   20 1

Ejercicio 5:   21A   22A   23B   24C   25C   26B   27A   28C   29B   30A

Section 2, Exercise 1:   1B   2C   3A   4A   5B

Ejercicio 2:   6 *carta*   7 *pariente*   8 *santa*   9 *extranjero*   10 *verano*
11 *acompañar*   12 *subir*   13 *impaciencia*

Ejercicio 3:   14B   15D   16F   17A   18C   19E   20G

Section 3, Ejercicio 1:   1 *Gerardo*   2 *Pedro*   3 *Alvaro*   4 *Rafael*   5 *Patricio*
6 *Sheila*   7 *Lolita*   8 *Ana*   9 *Maite*   10 *Esteban*

Ejercicio 2:   11A   12E   13D   14C   15B

Ejercicio 3:   16 *en el hospital*   17 *fin de curso*   18 *para limpiar los cristales*   19 *seda*
20 *la comida*   21 *el olor del río*   22 *en la montaña*   23 *comen las ovejas*
24 *su velocidad*   25 *45*

Exercise 4:   26A   27C   28C   29A   30B

Appendix

LISTENING CHAPTER TRANSCRIPT

Section 1: Foundation

EXERCISE 1: *A Spanish girl is speaking about her plans for the weekend. Answer briefly in English. Who is coming?*

Girl: Mi amiga viene esta tarde.

The correct answer is her friend.

Question one. Where are they going?

Girl: Vamos al cine.

Question two. How will they travel?

Girl: Cogemos el autobús.

Question three. What time does it start?

Girl: La película empieza a las ocho.

Question four. How much does it cost?

Girl: Para estudiantes, son cuatrocientas pesetas.

Question five. When are they going to the disco?

Girl: Vamos a la discoteca mañana.

EJERCICIO 2: ¿Dónde estás?

Woman: Quiero dos kilos de naranjas y uno de plátanos.

Man: La respuesta correcta es B. Pregunta número uno

Woman: Déme una barra de pan; dos panecillos y un pastel.

Man: Pregunta número dos

Boy: Quiero un kilo de salchichas y un pollo.

Man: Pregunta número tres

Girl: Me gusta la chaqueta gris. Pero, . . .no, prefiero los pantalones.

Man: Pregunta número cuatro

Boy: Entonces, dos sellos . . .y ¿para mandar una carta a Francia? ¿Cuánto es?

Man: Pregunta número cinco

Girl: Voy a comprar gasolina y un mapa.

EJERCICIO 3: Antonio describe la ciudad.
¿De qué habla?

Man: Si quieres hacer turismo, el pueblo está bastante cerca.

Woman: La respuesta correcta es B. Pregunta número uno

Man: La plaza mayor es un sitio interesante, pero un poco turístico.

Woman: Pregunta número dos

Man: Si quieres salir de excursión, ve a la estación de autocares.

Woman: Pregunta número tres

Man: Tienes que vistar la catedral antigua.

Woman: Pregunta número cuatro

Man: Y, muy cerca, se vende todo tipo de comida en el mercado.

Woman: Pregunta número cinco

Man: Y ¿para cambiar dinero?

EJERCICIO 4
Estás solo o sola en casa de tu amigo español. Suena el teléfono. Tú tomas un recado para el padre de tu amigo.

Haz unos apuntes en español.

Man: ¿No está el señor Casal? ¿Le puede decir que le han Ilamado de la agencia de viajes?

Woman: La respuesta correcta es la agencia de viajes.

Man: Bueno, le dejo un recado, ¿vale? Yo soy Martín Villalba. Soy jefe de la agencia. Sólo hay billetes para el señor y su mujer. El día 23 es fiesta, entonces tienen que viajar el día siguiente. El avión sale a las 07.35. El vuelo dura una hora. Podemos reservar el billete si el señor nos da el número de su tarjeta de crédito.

Section 2: Common

EXERCISE 5: *You listen to a recorded message at your penfriend's house. Where is the caller phoning from?*

Boy: Soy el amigo de Oscar. Les llamo desde el hospital.

The correct answer is hospital.

Boy: Oscar ha tenido un accidente. Todavía no hemos visto al médico. Llevamos una hora esperando. Parece que se ha roto la pierna. Además le duele mucho la espalda. Un camión enorme chocó con su bicicleta. El accidente ocurrió en los semáforos de la carretera de Cáceres.

EXERCISE 6

You will hear excerpts from a doctor and her patients. Questions 1–4. What medical problem is mentioned? Question 5. What advice is given?

Number 1

Man: Sí, me duele mucho el estómago. Ayer tuvimos una fiesta en casa y comí mucho. Creo que el pescado fue el origen del problema.

Number 2

Boy: Doctora, tengo dolor de cabeza . . . casi todos los días . . . Tomo aspirinas pero no me quitan totalmente el dolor.

Number 3

Girl: Estaba preparando la comida. He cogido el cuchillo pero . . . se me ha caído . . . y me he cortado la mano. La sangre no para.

Number 4

Man: Bueno a veces no veo muy bien. El otro día me equivoqué de autobús porque ¡no distinguía el número! Y . . . no me gusta llevar gafas.

Number 5

Girl: Con la fiebre que tienes, deberías guardar cama. No puedes volver al trabajo.

EJERCICO 7: En la radio: el pronóstico del tiempo.

Escribe la letra que corresponde. No necesitarás todas las letras.

Girl: Hoy habrá mucha nieve en los Pirineos. También va a hacer frío.

Woman: Las respuestas correctas son F y E

Número uno

Man: En Sevilla hará calor: se registrarán las temperaturas máximas . . . pero más tarde habrá vientos fuertes.

Número dos

Man: Para San Sebastián, cielos nublados con riesgo de lluvia por la tarde.

Número tres

Man: En Madrid capital, hará sol todo el día, pero esta noche habrá temperaturas muy bajas.

Número cuatro

Man: Va a nevar en Pamplona y ¡cuidado! Esta noche habrá niebla en la zona.

EJERCICIO 8
Escucha a unos estudiantes españoles que hablan de su futuro.

Mira la lista de descripciones. Escucha y escribe la letra que corresponde. No necesitarás todas las letras.

Manuel: Soy Manuel. Me encanta el fútbol. Me entreno tres veces a la semana y juego todos los domingos. Voy a jugar en un club famoso.

Man: La respuesta correcta es C. Escucha a los jóvenes.

Susana: Me llamo Susana. Quiero ser médica de ancianos. Trabajo en una residencia de jubilados durante las vacaciones. Quiero estudiar medicina.

Yolanda: Me llamo Yolanda. Me gusta trabajar en el ordenador. Me gusta escribir cartas y preparar informes, como hacemos en la clase de informática.

Alvaro: Soy Alvaro. Me interesa pintar la naturaleza. También me gusta hacer dibujos. Cuando termine mis estudios, me gustaría ganarme la vida haciendo este tipo de cosas.

Patricia: Me llamo Patricia. Mi ambición consiste en hacerme millionaria. Para lograrlo, voy a hacerme vendedora de productos de lujo.

Jaime: Soy Jaime. Paso muchas horas reparando coches. Siempre me han interesado mucho las máquinas. Yo espero encontrar trabajo en un taller.

Section 3: Higher

EJERCICIO 9: En la radio.
¿De qué se habla?

Woman: Esta mañana llegó al aeropuerto de Madrid el Presidente de los Estados Unidos. Empieza su visita a nuestro país.

Man: La respuesta correcta es: E

Número uno

Woman: Ocho muertos y más de veinte heridos es el balance provisional de una colisión grave en la autopista M30.

Número dos

Woman: ¿Entrenarse de forma seria, o practicar algo nuevo? Bueno, les podemos aconsejar sobre instalaciones deportivas, clases de baile …y mucho más.

Número tres

Woman: La Compañia de Electricidad creará otros doscientos empleos en el año próximo.

Número cuatro

Woman: Cuba ofrece al visitante sol, playas, música. En La Habana descubrirá una ciudad muy hermosa. La mayoriá de sus edificios son modernos...

Número cinco

Woman: Un portavoz del equipo nacional ha anunciado hoy que el jugador Martín, se ha recuperado y participará en el partido de esta tarde.

Número seis

Woman: Según el sindicato, los directores y los empleados de la RENFE han encontrado una solución a los problemas que paralizaron los trenes el día dos.

Número siete

Woman: Los soldados españoles llegaron en el siglo dieciséis. Al principio no atacaron. Más tarde murieron muchos españoles. Otros llevaron oro de México.

Número ocho

Woman: Se busca al señor Roberto González. Salió de su casa el día 3 y no ha vuelto. Tiene setenta años. Llevaba un traje gris y una camisa azul. Mide un metro ochenta y tiene los ojos castaños.

Número nueve

Woman: Al cabo de dos meses buscando, el enamorado, Luis, ha encontrado de nuevo a la chica de sus sueños. La habia conocido en el bar Lee.

Número diez

Woman: Buenas noticias para un o una habitante de Granada. El billete ganador del gran premio de 200 millones de pesetas se vendío en nuestra región.

EJERCICIO 10: Estas personas han visto unas películas.

Woman: Estoy segura de que esta película se llevará un premio. Es una obra maravillosa.

La letra correcta es L.

Número uno

Girl: Voy a decir a todos mis amigos que vengan a ver esta película.

Número dos

Woman: No tenía nada de interés. Y tú ¡Estabas dormido! Al menos no roncabas.

Número tres

Girl: ¡Qué vida más trágica! Era insoportable. ¡ Al final, lloré!

Número cuatro

Woman: A mis nietos les encantó, . . . incluso al más pequeño que tenía solo tres años.

Número cinco

Girl: Yo no quería venir. ¿Era necesario representar tanta brutalidad . . . peleas y también concentrarse en la sangre?

Número seis

Woman: Bueno, en mi opinión, la película no es apta para menores. La he prohibido a mi hijo.

Número siete

Girl: Para mí resultó difícil seguir el argumento. Me parece difícil de entender.

Número ocho

Woman: No merece la pena hacer cola. ¡Era rídícula y además tontísima!

Número nueve

Girl: ¡Qué risa! Es la película más divertida del año. Me reí muchísimo.

Número diez

Woman: La película describe cómo vivía la gente en tiempos pasados durante el siglo dieciocho.

EXERCISE 11: *You hear Ramón talking to a friend about his job.*

What is Ramón's job?

Ramón: Bueno, sí, María, sigo siendo ingeniero electrónico.

The correct answer is: electronic engineer.

Ramón: Te lo juro, María, no aguanto más. Estoy harto de todo esto. Yo he hecho todo lo posible para arreglar las cosas. Y siempre el jefe me pide algo más.

Cuando la empresa se trasladó a Valencia, pues, yo también me mudé y sufri todos los problemas de cambiar de casa, aunque a mis padres no les gustó nada la idea. Y, al llegar, acepté un puesto con una responsabilidad importante sin suplemento de paga. Y ahora… eljefe quiere mandarme a trabajar en el extranjero. No sabe ni siquiera si hablo otros idiomas. De hecho, tengo conocimientos de inglés y de francés. Pero, ¡no voy a decírselo!

SPEAKING CHAPTER TRANSCRIPT

Role play 1: Section 1: Foundation

CARD 1

Examiner: Estás en un café. Yo soy el/la camarero/a*. Hola. ¿Qué vais a tomar?

Candidate: Un café con leche, por favor.

E: ¿Algo más ?

C: Agua mineral, por favor.

E: ¿Y de comer?

C: Patatas, por favor.

E: Muy bien.

C: ¿Dónde están los servicios?

E: Al fondo, a la derecha.

(*depends on gender of speaker*)

CARD 2

Examiner: Estás en un albergue juvenil. Hablas con el/la empleado/a*. Hola, buenas tardes.

Candidate: ¿Hay camas, por favor?

E: ¿Para cuántas personas?

C: Somos dos.

E: ¿Para cuántas noches?

C: Una noche.

E: Sí, tenemos camas.

C: ¿Cuánto cuestan?

E: Son novecientas pesetas la noche.

CARD 3

Examiner: Yo trabajo en un estanco. Hola, buenos días. ¿Qué quieres?

Candidate: Postales, por favor.

E: Aquí están. ¿Algo más?

C: Sellos, por favor.

E: ¿Para dónde?

C: Para Francia.

E: Muy bien.

C: ¿Cuánto es?

E: Son ciento ochenta pesetas.

Role play 2: Section 2: Common (Foundation and Higher)

CARD 1
Examiner: Trabajas en un restaurante. Hablas con un/a amigo/a. Yo soy el/la amigo/a*. Bueno. Háblame de tu trabajo de fin de semana.

Candidate: Empiezo a las nueve.

E: ¿Como es el restaurante?

C: El restaurante es moderno y cómodo.

E: ¿Qué haces exactamente?

C: Lavo los platos.

E: En tu trabajo, ¿cuánto ganas por semana?

C: Cuarenta libras.

E: No está mal.

CARD 2
Examiner: Estás con tu familia en España y tenéis un accidente. Llamas a los servicios de urgencia. Yo trabajo allí. Urgencias. Dígame.

Candidate: Me llamo Sam Jones. Hemos tenido un accidente.

E: ¿Qué marca de coche es? ¿De qué color es?

C: Es un Fiat rojo.

E: ¿Los pasajeros están bien?

C: Una persona está herida.

E: Bueno. La ambulancia estará pronto ahí. ¿Quién es la persona herida?

C: Es mi hermano.

E: Hasta pronto. Adiós.

CARD 3
Examiner: Yo soy tu amigo/a español/a y acabo de llegar a tu casa. ¿Dónde voy a dormir?

Candidate: Tu habitación está arriba.

E: Ah, gracias.

C: ¿Qué te gusta comer?

E: Como de todo.

C: ¿Quieres ir a la discoteca?

E: ¡Sí, me gustaría mucho ir!

C: ¿A qué hora vas a la cama normalmente?

E: A las once.

C: Vale.

Role play 3: Section 3: Higher

CARD 1

Examiner: Cuéntame lo que pasó durante tu estancia en España.

Candidate: Pues el verano pasado trabajé en España en un hotel en Torremolinos. Pasé dos semanas allí y me divertí mucho. Era un hotel de tres estrellas y era bastante cómodo.

E: ¿Cuántas habitaciones había?

C: Había sesenta habitaciones y había una piscina enorme. El hotel organizaba actividades de toda clase para los clientes. Se podía hacer ciclismo, equitación, deportes, juegos y había hasta un teatro. Por la tarde había espectáculos, bailes y concursos. En mi opinión era un hotel excelente porque ofrecía tantas cosas que hacer.

E: Y ¿nadaste en la piscina?

C: Sí, nadaba todos los días antes de empezar a trabajar. Yo tenía una habitación en el hotel. Era muy pequeña pero era cómoda. Me levantaba a las siete, tomaba el desayuno y empezaba a trabajar. A la una tenía dos horas libres y normalmente iba a la playa o iba de compras. Mi trabajo terminaba a las cinco de la tarde y podía tomar una ducha y salir con mis amigos. Había mucho que hacer y me gustaba la ciudad. Me acostaba a las diez.

E:- Y ¿el trabajo?

C: El trabajo no era muy interesante. Tenía que hacer las camas, pasar la aspiradora y poner las mesas. A veces trabajaba en el bar y eso era mucho más interesante sobre todo cuando los clientes bebían demasiado Eso ocurrió muchas veces. Trabajaba ocho horas cada día y al final del día estaba cansada.

E: – ¿Había otras cosas que hacer?

C: – A veces había problemas con las duchas, las llaves y las ventanas. Yo ayudaba a reparar las cosas estropeadas. A veces había problemas con los clientes. Algunos no podían pagar la cuenta porque habían gastado todo su dinero en el bar.

E: Y ¿en tu tiempo libre?

C: Yo iba a la playa. Conocí a muchos españoles e íbamos a los clubs y a los restaurantes juntos. En mi día libre tomé un autocar y fui visitar todos los monumentos históricos de la región. Vi la catedral y un castillo viejo.

CARD 2

Candidate: El año pasado mi instituto organizó un intercambio con un instituto en España y en junio yo fui a España. Viajé a Málaga en la costa y la familia era muy simpática y generosa.

Examiner: Y ¿qué hiciste el primer día?

C: – El primer día fui al instituto en autocar. Hacía sol y mucho calor.

E: — ¿Qué tal las clases?

C: — Las clases empezaban a las nueve y eran todas muy interesantes. Durante la clase de inglés tuve que hablar delante de la clase. Fue muy divertido. En mi opinión el instituto era muy moderno y los alumnos y profesores eran todos muy simpáticos.

E: — Qué hacías los fines de semana?

C: — Dabamos paseos por el campo y un domingo fuimos a esquiar a la montaña.

E: – Y ¿los sábados?

C: Un sábado hubo una fiesta enorme con todos los estudiantes del instituto. La comida era excelente pero desgraciadamente comí demasiado y tuve dolor de estomágo.

CARD 3

Candidate: El día de mi cumpleaños me levanté a las ocho y tomé un desayuno excelente de huevos fritos y cereales. A las nueve el cartero trajo muchos regalos.

Examiner: Qué regalos recibiste?

C: Recibí un ordenador de parte de mis tíos, dinero de parte de mis abuelos, y una cámara fotográfica de parte de mi hermana en Australia. Luego fui de compras con mis amigos. Fuimos a pie al centro comercial y compré mucha comida y bebida para la fiesta.

E: — ¿A qué hora era la fiesta?

C: — A las nueve, pero primero hubo una cena especial y mis primos vinieron y cenamos juntos.

E: — ¿Qué comisteis?

C: — Cominos mucho pollo asado con patatas y también un pastel. Luego mis amigos llegaron y las fiesta tuvo lugar en la sala de estar. Mis padres salieron y pudimos bailar, comer, beber y charlar.

E: — ¿Te gustó la fiesta?

C: — En mi opinión la fiesta fue excelente porque habiá mucho que comer y beber, la música estuvo muy bien y todos mis amigos estuvieron allí.

E: – Y ¿después?

C: – Mis padres volvieron a las doce y mis amigos se marcharon. Yo tuve que arreglar la casa y desgraciadamente tuve que lavar los platos.

Candidate 1 – Foundation

PRESENTATION AND DISCUSSION: *EL FÚTBOL*

Candidate: Voy a hablar de mi deporte favorito, el fútbol. Vivo en Londres y mi equipo favorito es el Chelsea. Veo los partidos en la tele y en mi habitación tengo fotos de los jugadores y otros recuerdos del club. También todos mis amigos y todas mis amigas son aficionados al Chelsea y durante el recreo hablamos del último partido y del próximo partido. Los jerseys del Chelsea son azules y el día de mi cumpleaños mis padres me regalaron un jersey azul y lo llevo todo el tiempo.

También me gusta jugar al fútbol y los sábados voy al parque con mis amigos y amigas y jugamos al fútbol y al tenis. Un día quisiera ser futbolista y jugar al fútbol para el Chelsea. Los futbolistas ganan mucho dinero y me gustaría ganar lo que ganan ellos.

Examiner: Y ¿cómo se llama el estadio del Chelsea?

C: Se llama Stamford Bridge. Yo vivo muy cerca. Vivo a un kilómetro de Stamford Bridge y los sábados hay mucho tráfico y mucha gente en nuestra calle.

E: Y ¿has visitado Stamford Bridge?

C: Sí, el año pasado fui con mi padre. Era un regalo especial porque había estudiado mucho. Mi padre tuvo que reservar las entradas cuatro semanas antes del partido. Me encantó el ambiente y no hubo problemas con los espectadores: no hubo violencia.

E: ¿Que pasó?

C: Desafortunadamente el Chelsea perdió uno a cero contra el Everton. Pero el partido estuvo muy interesante. Creo que el árbitro era muy malo. El Everton no jugó bien pero marcó un gol afortunado.

E: ¿Por qué no vas más a ver al Chelsea?

C: Porque cuesta demasiado dinero. Una entrada cuesta treinta libras y si vas en un grupo cuesta mucho. Mi padre dice que no es posible.

E: ¿Qué haces entonces?

C: Veo los partidos en la televisión. Los sábados por la tarde siempre veo el fútbol.

E: Y ¿juegas al fútbol en un equipo?

C: Antes jugaba para un equipo pero no tenía bastante tiempo para entrenarme así que no lo hago más. Prefiero jugar con amigos en el parque. Es más divertido y menos peligroso.

E: ¿Haces otros deportes?

C: Sí, me gusta el tenis y juego con mi hermana. Ella es mayor que yo y siempre gana. También juego con amigos. Y veo tenis en la tele. Me gusta ver Wimbledon todos los años.

E: Bueno ahora vamos a hablar de tu instituto. ¿Eres alumno en qué tipo de instituto? ¿Cuántos alumnos hay?

C: Es un instituto mixto y hay mil alumnos.

E: Describe tu instituto.

C: Mi instituto es moderno y muy grande. Hay laboratorios, canchas de tenis, campos deportivos y una biblioteca enorme. También hay un ambiente agradable. Para los mil alumnos, más o menos, hay sesenta profesores y profesoras. El instituto acaba de comprar treinta ordenadores nuevos, todos con Internet. Podemos usar los ordenadores después del fin de las clases hasta las nueve de la noche. También podermos usarlos desde las siete de la mañana.

E: ¿Las clases empiezan y terminan a qué hora?

C: Empiezan a las nueve y terminan a las tres y media. También tenemos una hora de comer y tengo la oportunidad de hacer mis deberes y hacer deportes.

E: ¿Cuáles son tus asignaturas favoritas? ¿Por qué?

C: Mis asignaturas favoritas son las lenguas porque quiero ser profesor de lenguas. Pero me gustan casi todas mis asignaturas. La asignatura que no me gusta es la historia porque la profesora es muy severa.

E: ¿Llevas uniforme? Describe tu uniforme. ¿Cuál es tu opinión de tu uniforme?

C: Sí, tengo que llevar uniforme. Es de color negro y as muy triste. No me gusta.

E: ¿Qué haces durante la hora de comer?

C: Charlo con mis amigos, como bocadillos y bebo coca cola.

E: ¿Practicas deportes en tu instituto? ¿Te gusta?

C: Juego al fútbol y al tenis y me gusta mucho.

E: Describe lo que hiciste ayer en tu instituto.

C: Ayer llegué a las nueve, fui a mis clases, hablé con mis amigos, comí mis bocadillos y volví a casa.

E: Describe lo que vas a hacer después de los exámenes. ¿Vas a seguir con tus estudios?

C: Voy a estudiar francés y español. Más tarde voy a estudiar en una universidad y un día quiero ser profesor.

E: Ahora vamos a hablar de tu región. ¿Dónde vives exactamente?

C: Vivo en Londres, la capital de Inglaterra en el sureste de Inglaterra. Vivo bastante cerca del centro y a veces voy de compras al centro con mi hermana.

E: ¿Desde hace cuántos años vives allí?

C: Vivo allí dieciséis años, es decir toda mi vida.

E: ¿Cómo es tu ciudad? ¿Te gusta?

C: Me gusta mucho, pero es demasiado grande. Hay muchos barrios que no conozco. Y hay demasiado tráfico. Pero la gente es simpática. Afortunadamente tengo muchos amigos y siempre hay algo que hacer. Pero también me gusta salir de Londres. Voy al campo, que no está lejos.

E: ¿Cuántos habitantes hay en Londres?

C: Hay ocho millones de habitantes más o menos. Hay muchas nacionalidades y muchos españoles. Mi mejor amigo es español y charlamos mucho en español.

E: ¿Qué se puede hacer para divertirse?

C: Se puede ir al cine, a patinar y se puede ir a ver espectáculos. A mi hermana le gusta ir de compras. También hay muchas oportunidades para practicar deportes.

E: Describe lo que hiciste cuando saliste por última vez.

C: Fui al cine con mis amigos. Fuimos a ver una película americana y después bebimos un zumo de fruta en un café. Charlamos y jugamos con los videojuegos. Me lo pasá bien.

E: ¿Qué harás esta noche?

C: Saldré con mis amigos. Iremos a un club donde hay buena música. Charlaremos, bailaremos, beberemos Coca Cola, escucharemos la música y lo pasaremos muy bien.

Candidate 2 – Higher

PRESENTATION AND DISCUSSION: *MI VISITA A ESPAÑA*

Candidate: Voy a hablar de una visita que hice el año pasado a España. Mis padres estaban hartos del tiempo en mayo en Inglaterra así que decidieron pasar un fin de semana en Málaga. Y yo les acompañé. Mi hermana también. Al llegar hacía buen tiempo y después de encontrar nuestro hotel de cuatro estrellas fuimos a la playa. Nadé en mar y jugué al baloncesto con unos españoles. Por la noche fuimos a un restaurante y comimos unos platos típicos – paella y sangría. Después mi hermana y yo fuimos a un club y bailamos hasta las cuatro de la madrugada. Al día siguiente, mi padre alquiló un coche e hicimos una excursión a la montaña. Las vistas eran magníficas. Fue un fin de semana inolvidable y volveré a Málaga el año que viene.

E: Y ¿qué hicisteis el segundo día?

C: Nos quedamos en Málaga. Fuimos de compras y compramos regalos para mis tíos y mis primos.

E: ¿Cuál es tu opinión de España?

C: Me encanta. Me encantan el clima y la comida pero sobre todo me gusta la gente.

E: ¿Por qué te gusta la gente?

C: Porque los españoles son tan simpáticos y generosos.

E: ¿Cuál es tu plato favorito?

C: Me gusta muchísimo la tortilla española. Mis padres prefieren el vino español.

E: Y cuando hiciste una excursión en coche alquilado, ¿dónde fuisteis?

C: Fuimos a Granada. El viaje duró dos horas porque hay una autopista maravillosa. En Granada vimos todos los monumentos históricos.

E: Y ¿qué hiciste en los clubs en Málaga?

C: Bailé mucho, charlé con muchas personas, comí patatas bravas y bebí zumo de fruta.

E: Y ¿el tiempo?

C: Hacía sol y calor todo el tiempo. Durante la noche hacía calor también.

E: Describe tu hotel.

C: Había muchas instalaciones muy atractivas. Había aire acondicionado, una terraza, un restaurante excelente y dos piscinas.

E: ¿Cómo viajaste a Málaga?

C: Tomamos un vuelo directo del aeropuerto de Manchester. Al llegar a Málaga, tomamos un taxi a nuestro hotel.

E: Y a tu hermana, ¿le gustaba España?

C: Sí, muchísimo. Conoció a un español que se llamaba Carlos y salieron juntos. Carlos le dio un regalo cuando nos marchamos.

E: ¿Qué regalo?

C: Le dio un florero de porcelana.

E: Describe a Carlos.

C: Carlos era muy guapo. Tenía los ojos marrones y el pelo negro. Llevaba ropa muy elegante.

E: Muy bien. Ahora vamos a hablar de tu trabajo y tu futuro. ¿Tienes un empleo? ¿Dónde trabajas?

C: Trabajo en una tienda durante el fin de semana?

E: ¿Cuántas horas trabajas a la semana?

C: Trabajo ocho horas los sábados y tres horas los domingos.

E: ¿Qué opinas de tu trabajo?

C: Me gusta mucho porque es interesante y gano mucho dinero.

E: ¿Qué experiencia de trabajo has hecho? ¿Qué hiciste exactamente?

C: Trabajé en una oficina. Tenía que contestar al teléfono y escribir cartas.

E: ¿Cuál es tu opinión de tu trabajo? ¿Era útil?

C: Sí, era útil porque aprendí mucho y conocí a mucha gente interesante.

E: ¿Qué aprendiste?

C: Aprendí a usar un ordenador y a llegar a la hora cada día.

E: ¿En qué quieres trabajar en el futuro?

C: Voy a ser médico.

E: ¿Por qué has escogido este trabajo?

C: Porque me gusta la idea de curar a los enfermos.

E: ¿Qué vas a hacer el año que viene?

C: Voy a seguir con mis estudios. Voy a estudiar inglés, francés y español.

E: Ahora vamos a hablar de tu instituto. Describe tu instituto – los edificios, el número de alumnos, etc.

C: Mi instituto es muy grande y muy moderno. Hay mil doscientos alumnos y es un instituto mixto. Hay setenta profesores, más o menos, y todos son muy simpáticos. Hay canchas de tenis, campos deportivos, laboratorios, un laboratorio de lenguas, una biblioteca enorme y muchas otras instalaciones.

E: ¿Qué asignaturas has escogido y por qué?

C: He escogido matemáticas, inglés, francés, español, ciencias, dibujo y religión. He escogido estas asignaturas porque en mi opinión son las mejores para mí.

E: ¿Cómo son los profesores en tu instituto? ¿Hay buenas relaciones entre los profesores y los alumnos?

C: Los profesores son simpáticos, inteligentes y trabajadores. Casi siempre hay buenas relaciones entre los profesores y los alumnos.

E: ¿Llevas uniforme? ¿Qué opinas?

C: Sí, tenemos que llevar uniforme. No me gusta el uniforme pero sé que es necesario.

E: ¿Cuáles son las ventajas y las desventajas de un uniforme?

C: La ventaja es que es barato y no tienes que decidir lo que te vas a poner. La desventaja es que el uniforme es triste y aburrido.

E: Describe lo que hiciste en tu instituto ayer.

C: Llegué a las nueve, fui a mis clases y charlé con mis amigos. Durante la hora de comer comí en la cantina luego fui a la hacer mis deberes con un ordenador. Volví a casa a las cuatro.

E: ¿Qué cosas te gustaría cambiar? ¿Por qué?

C: Me gustaría cambiar la comida en la cantina porque es muy mala.

E: ¿Qué vas a hacer después de tus exámenes?

C: Voy a ir de vacaciones con mis padres. Iremos a Alemania.

E: ¿Cuáles son tus ambiciones?

C: Mi ambición es ser muy rica y tener una casa enorme.

E: ¿Tus años en el instituto te han preparado bien para la vida? ¿Por qué?

C: Sí me han preparado mucho porque con lo que he aprendido voy a conseguir un buen trabajo.

Candidate 3 – Higher

PRESENTATION AND DISCUSSION: *MI EXPERIENCIA DEL TRABAJO*

Candidate: Voy a hablar de la semana que pasé trabajando en un hotel en el centro de mi ciudad. Estaba a cinco minutos de mi casa. Mi instituto organizó la semana y me divertí mucho. Tenía que llegar a las siete de la mañana, así que me levantaba a las seis. Esto era dificilísimo. En el hotel el patrón era muy simpático y me ayudó mucho. A las siete tenía que ayudar con el desayuno. Tenía que traer la comida y la bebida a los clientes. Luego tenía que limpiar las habitaciones y a mediodía trabajaba en el bar, sirviendo las bebidas. Y a las tres volvía a casa. Durante la semana gané veinte libras en propinas. Fue una experiencia maravillosa y muy útil.

Examiner: ¿Cómo viajaste al hotel?

C: Fui a pie.

E: Describe el hotel.

C: El hotel era bastante grande con treinta habitaciones. No había piscina, pero había una peluquería, bares y un restaurante.

E: Y describe al patrón.

C: El patrón era un señor de cuarenta años de edad, más o menos. Era bastante alto y muy delgado. Era casi calvo. Siempre llevaba un traje y era muy cortés.

E: Y el desayuno en el hotel, ¿ tenías que preparar la comida?

C: No, había un cocinero que preparaba la comida. Yo tenía que recibir a los clientes y preguntarles lo que querían comer y beber. Era casi siempre igual. Querían desayuno completo con té. Luego tenía que traer el desayuno a las mesas.

E: Y cuando limpiabas las habitaciones, ¿qué tenías que hacer?

C: Tenía que cambiar las sábanas, pasar la aspiradora y arreglar la habitacíon.

E: Y cuando estabas en el bar, ¿qué tenías que hacer?

C: Tenía que abrir las botellas y traer las bebidas a las menas de los clientes.

E: ¿Te gustaba el trabajo?

C: Sí, me gustaba mucho. Era muy interesante y conocí a mucha gente. Y también gané un poco de dinero. Lo que me gustaba era el ambiente agradable en el hotel. Lo que no me gustaba era el humo en el bar donde tenía que trabajar. Muchos de los clientes fumaban y el humo me molesta.

E: Ahora vamos a hablar de tu tiempo libre. ¿Qué haces normalmente cuando estás libre por la tarde o durante el fin de semana?

C: Por la tarde veo la tele, escucho música, leo libros, juego con el ordenador y salgo con mis amigos. Durante el fin de semana hago deportes, voy a clubs con mis amigos y amigas y lo paso bien.

E: Habla de tu pasatiempo favorito. ¿Lo haces desde cuándo?

C: Me gusta el tenis. Juego al tenis desde hace cinco años. Me gusta porque es un deporte que es popular con los chicos y las chicas. Soy miembro de un club y voy al club una vez a la semana.

E: ¿Te gustan los deportes? ¿Por qué?

C: Me gustan casi todos los deportes. El deporte que no me gusta es el boxeo porque es demasiado violento.

E: ¿Cuántas horas al día ves la tele?

C: Veo la tele dos o tres horas al día.

E: ¿Qué tipo de programa te gusta? ¿Por qué?

C: Me gustan las telenovelas. Me gustan porque aprendo mucho de lo que pasa en la vida.

E: ¿Te gusta la música? ¿Qué clase?

C: Sí, me encanta la música, sobre todo la música pop.

E: ¿Tocas un instrumento musical?

C: Toco la guitarra. En el pasado tocaba el piano pero no me gustaba.

E: Habla de lo que hiciste el fin de semana pasado.

C: El fin de semana pasado, fui de compras con una amiga. Compré regalos para mi familia, luego fuimos al cine. Después, volvimos a casa y vi la tele. El domingo di un paseo en el campo con el perro.

E: ¿Cuáles son tus planes para el fin de semana que viene?

C: Voy a ir a una fiesta el sábado por la tarde. Primero iré al centro de la ciudad a comprar cosas para la fiesta. Compraré ropa nueva y regalos. El domingo visitaré a mis abuelos.

E: Si tuvieras mucho dinero, ¿qué deporte o actividad te gustaría practicar?

C: Si gano la lotería, quiero hacer vela. Parece un deporte muy atractivo. Me gustaría también tener un avión!

E: Ahora vamos a hablar de tus vacaciones. ¿Dónde prefieres pasar tus vacaciones y con quién?

C: Prefiero ir a Francia con mi familia.

E: ¿Cómo prefieres viajar y por qué?

C: Prefiero ir en avión porque es más rápido.

E: ¿Dónde fuiste de vacaciones el año pasado?

C: Fui a Francia con mi familia.

E: Habla de tus vacaciones del año pasado. ¿Dónde te quedaste? ¿Con quién? ¿Qué hiciste?

C: Fuimos al noroeste de Francia con una caravana. Nos quedamos en un camping muy cómodo y moderno. Durante el día tomamos el sol, nadamos en la piscina, leímos, escuchamos música y comimos y bebimos mucho. Durante la tarde fuimos a la discoteca.

E: ¿La vida en Francia es muy distinta de la vida en Gran Bretaña?

C: Sí, es muy distinta. La comida es mejor, el clima es mejor y tienen más tiempo libre.

E: ¿Qué te gustaba más en Francia?

C: Me gustaba más el clima. Hace más calor y no llueve todo el tiempo como en Inglaterra.

E: ¿Quieres volver? ¿Por qué?

C: Sí, quiero volver porque ahora tengo muchos amigos y amigas en Francia.

E: ¿Tienes planes para el verano que viene? ¿Dónde irás?

C: Iremos a España. Viajaremos en avión y nos quedaremos en un hotel en la costa. Nadaremos y tomaremos el sol todos los días.

E: Describe tus vacaciones ideales.

C: Me gustaría viajar por los Estados Unidos en coche visitando todos los sitios de interés.

PRACTICE EXAMINATION LISTENING

Section 1 : Foundation

EXERCISE 1: *You arrive at Madrid airport and ask the best way to get to the city centre.*

Man: ¿El centro? Toma un autobús.

The correct answer is B.

Question 1: You ask someone the way to the Hotel Sol. Which way should you go?

Man: ¿El hotel Sol? Tienes que ir a la izquierda.

Question 2: In the hotel you ask the price of a room. What is the reply?

Woman: Una habitación cuesta cinco mil quinientas pesetas.

Question 3: What facility in your room are you told about?

Woman: Su habitación tiene una ducha.

Question 4: You want to know what time the restaurant opens. What is the reply?

Man: El restaurante abre a las ocho y media.

Question 5: What problem are you told about?

Man: Lo siento, el ascensor no funciona.

EJERCICIO 2: Ana habla de su familia.

¿Cuántos años tiene Ana?

Ana: Hola. Me llamo Ana. Tengo 16 años.

La respuesta correcta es B.

Pregunta 6:

Ana: Tengo una hermana y dos hermanos.

Pregunta 7:

Ana: También tenemos un conejo en casa. Se llama Enrique.

Pregunta 8:

Ana: Mi padre es cocinero.

Pregunta 9:

Ana: Mi madre es médico.

Pregunta 10:

Ana: Los fines de semana me gusta bailar.

Pregunta 11:

Ana: En mi colegio, mi asignatura favorita es química.

Pregunta 12:

Ana: Cuando el colegio termina, vuelvo a casa a pie.

Pregunta 13:

Ana: Vivo en una casa en el campo.

Pregunta 14:

Ana: Ayudo a mis padres. Siempre lavo los platos.

Pregunta 15:

Ana: Por la tarde me gusta leer.

EJERCICIO 3

¿Dónde está Paco?

Paco: Estoy en casa y veo la tele.

La respuesta correcta es A.

Pregunta 16:

Paco: Voy a ver una película.

Pregunta17:

Paco: Paso mis vacaciones en Inglaterra.

Pregunta 18:

Paco: Dormimos en una tienda.

Pregunta 19:

Paco: Estoy comprando sellos en la oficina de Correos.

Pregunta 20:

Paco: Vamos a visitar una torre famosa.

EJERCICIO 4

Siete jóvenes hablan de cómo ayudan en casa.

Marco: Me llamo Marco. Los sábados lavo el coche.

Le letra correcta es A.

Pregunta 21:

Ana: Me llamo Ana. Ayudo a mis padres pasando la aspiradora.

Pregunta 22:

Luis: Me llamo Luis. Trabajo mucho en el jardín.

Pregunta 23:

Cristina: Me llamo Cristina. Siempre hago mi cama.

Pregunta 24:

José: Me llamo José. Lavo la ropa en mi casa.

Pregunta 25:

David: Me llamo David. Yo preparo todas las comidas.

EJERCICIO 5: Isabel describe el pueblo. ¿De qué habla?

Isabel: Mira el estadio de fútbol.

La respuesta correcta es A.

Pregunta 26:

Isabel: En el centro está la iglesia de San Juan.

Pregunta 27:

Isabel: Al lado hay un supermercado enorme.

Pregunta 28:

Isabel: En la calle mayor hay muchas tiendas interesantes.

Pregunta 29:

Isabel: El ayuntamiento es un lugar famoso.

Pregunta 30:

Isabel: Muy cerca está la estación de ferrocarriles.

Section 2: Common

EXERCISE 1: *Lolita is talking about what she did last night.*

Lolita: Trabajo en un supermercado.

Number 1.

Lolita: A las seis de la tarde volví de mi trabajo. ¡Me dolía tanto la cabeza!

Number 2.

Lolita: Pero a las ocho me sentía mucho mejor. Tomé un baño y el dolor desapareció.

Number 3.

Lolita: Miré en la nevera . . . nada. ¡Tenía tante hambre!

Number 4.

Lolita: Llamé por teléfono a reservar una mesa en El Tulipán.

Number 5

Lolita: Al llegar ¡qué suerte! Vi que mi amigo Rafael ya estaba ahí. Cenamos juntos.

EJERCICIO 2: Escucha a estos españoles hablando de su futuro.

Rocío: Me llamo Rocío. Me encanta el baloncesto y mis amigos dicen que soy la mejor del equipo. Quiero jugar en un club en los Estados Unidos.

La respuesta correcta es D.

Alvaro: Me llamo Alvaro. Pasé las vacaciones en un hospital. Pero no cuidaba a los pacientes. Prepara las comidas en la cantina y esta será mi profesión futura.

María: Me llamo María. Me entiendo bien con los jóvenes y tengo una idea clara de lo que voy a hacer. Voy a enseñar.

Clara: Me llamo Clara. Mi asignatura favorita es la informática y paso mucho tiempo mejorando mis habilidades.

Susi: Me llamo Susi. Escribo artículos para una revista y un día quiero hacer algo igual, trabajando en los medios de comunicación.

Carlos: Me llamo Carlos. Me interesan los edificios y quiero crear diseños interesantes y un centro de ciudad futurístico.

Pedro: Me llamo Pedro. Tengo muchos talentos y no me importa lo que voy a hacer. Lo importante es ver y trabajar en muchos países del mundo.

Jaime: Me llamo Jaime. Me encanta la historia de mi país. Voy a estudiarla mucho, luego voy a escribir libros sobre ella.

EJERCICIO 3: En la radio: el pronóstico del tiempo

Woman: Hoy va a llover en Madrid. También hará frio.

En Barcelona habrá sol y temperaturas muy altas.

En Cádiz, cielos nubosos con vientos fuertes.

En Santiago, habrá nieve y hielo en las carreteras.

En Málaga, tormentas con relámpagos y truenos.

Section 3: Higher

EJERCICIO 1: En la radio. ¿De qué se habla?

Man: Buenos días, radioyentes. Ahora las noticias.

Woman: Un tren con destino a Madrid chocó con un camión en un paso a nivel. Hubo cuatro muertos.

La respuesta correcta es B.

1. **Woman:** El Rey de España habló hoy con el primer ministro de Inglaterra sobre los problemas de los pescadores españoles.

2. **Woman:** Joyas valoradas en diez millones de pesetas desaparecieron de la caja fuerta de un banco en Sevilla.

3. **Woman:** Un terremoto en China ha provocado millares de muertos.

4. **Woman:** La madre de la reina de Inglaterra hoy cumplió cien años. Los británicos declararon un día de fíesta.

5. **Woman:** Gran alegría en Canarias. Casi toda la población de un pueblo en las montañas son ahora millonarios.

6. **Woman:** Todos los empleados de RENFE se negaron a trabajar hoy por problemas de sueldo.

7. **Woman:** Según el ministerio de turismo, habrá cinco mil nuevos empleos en las costas este año.

8. **Woman:** El famoso futbolista británico Joe Johnson y su mujer van a divorciarse.

9. **Woman:** La estrella de la película *Amor en Chicago* dio a luz hoy a un niño. Es su cuarto.

10. **Woman:** El Madrid gaño anoche en Málaga. Ahora son campeones.

EJERCICIO 2: Un español describe su vida en Nueva York.

Woman: ¿Dónde vives exactamente?

Francisco: Vivo en el centro.

La respuesta correcta es B.

Woman: ¿Qué tal Nueva York, Francisco?

Francisco: Me encuentro bien aquí en Nueva York. Hay tanto trabajo y mucha gente habla español.

Woman: ¿Cúando llegaste a Nueva York?

Francisco: Cuando tenía dieciséis años, es decir, hace veinte años. Tuve que dejar a mi familia pues no había trabajo en España. Llegué solo pero ahora estoy casado.

Woman: ¿En qué trabajas?

Francisco: Al llegar aquí, trabajé para un hombre muy rico. Cuidaba sus céspedes, sus plantas, sus flores y todo. Luego le mataron en la calle por su reloj de oro. Y yo perdí mi trabajo.

Woman: ¿Tienes ganas de volver a España?

Francisco: Cuando tenga bastante dinero. No quiero volver a la pobreza de España. Tengo amigos y contactos aquí.

Woman: ¿La violencia aquí en Nueva York es un problema?

Francisco: Pues en mi opinión no es peor ni mejor que las ciudades de España. Y para mí no es un problema porque nunca salgo por la noche.

EJERCICIO 3: Felipe habla de su empleo de vacaciones.

Felipe: En total trabajé un mes.

Yo quería trabajar en un bar. No quería trabajar en un hotel pero mis padres creyeron que sería mejor. Claro que tuve que hacer lo que mis padres quisieron.

La primera semana fue durante las vacaciones escolares y el hotel estaba siempre completo. Pero la segunda semana el hotel estaba vacío y me aburría tanto. No estoy contento cuando no tengo nada que hacer.

En la tercera semana todo cambió. Había una recepcionista, Reyes, que me hablaba mucho. Luego un día de la tercera semana dijo que quería salir conmigo. Puedes imaginarte mi respuesta.

En la cuarta semana el patrón dijo que Reyes había robado algo y Reyes tuvo que marcharse. Le dije al patrón que ya no podía trabajar para él y me fui.

EXERCISE 4: *A young man is having problems with his girlfriend*

Young man: Llevo dos años saliendo con Carmen.

Mis padres han alquilado un apartamento en la costa para el verano pero no quiero ir. Será la primera vez que no me marcho de vacaciones con mis padres. Pero es que tengo que ir a los Estados Unidos a aprender inglés. Mi novia, Carmen, está furiosa. Cuando le diji que iba a pasar las vacaciones sin ella dijo que no quería salir más conmigo. Dijo que cuando tenemos una cita yo siempre llego tarde. Y dice que siempre paga todo y que nunca comparto los gastos. Mucho de lo que dice es verdad. Mis padres tienen dinero, pero yo no. Así que no puedo pagar cuando salimos. Y es verdad que la puntualidad es un gran problema para mí. Pero creo que lo de pasar las vacaciones sin ella no es mi culpa. Tengo que aprender inglés y no hay más remedio. Para solucionar la situación fui a su casa con un ramo de rosas – doce. Al pasar delante de su casa esta mañana, vi que las flores estaban en el cubo de la basura.